"This slim volume . . . will be deeply appreciated by many who are waiting for a heart-warming, soul-searching word about the grace offered freely in Jesus Christ; a grace that can literally fashion us into 'new creatures.' "

—From the foreword by
Bishop James Armstrong
Resident Bishop
Dakotas Area
United Methodist Church

1

OUR
METHODIST
HERITAGE

Charles W. Keysor

David C. Cook Publishing Co.
850 NORTH GROVE AVENUE • ELGIN, IL 60120
In Canada: David C. Cook Publishing (Canada) Ltd., Weston, Ontario M9L 1T4

To my wife Marg, the ideal
Methodist wife and mother

CONTENTS

Preface

J. B. PHILLIPS, the English Bible expert, once said that working with the Gospels and Epistles of the New Testament is like grabbing hold of a bare electric wire.

This is the feeling I have about John and Charles Wesley. As a new Christian, converted at age 35, I began singing Charles Wesley's hymns and reading about John Wesley. In them I have always found exciting vitality—a clean-cut muscular faith that reminds me of the Acts of the Apostles . . . of Ephesians . . . of Matthew, Mark, Luke, and John.

My respect for original Methodism grew through studies under Drs. Philip Watson and Frederick Norwood at Garrett Theological Seminary. My appreciation was reinforced by almost a decade of agony and ecstasy as a local church pastor. And I am convinced that Scriptural Christianity of the Wesleys—like that of Calvin and Luther—is the only kind really worth having.

Original Methodism was like a rope composed of many strands. One was "conversion" or the "new birth." Another was "nurture" or growing in Christian faith and maturity. Another was the "priesthood of all believers"—fellow Christians in an intimate community, ministering to one another in the name and Spirit of Jesus.

Another historic Methodist strand was the central importance of Holy Communion, a continuing remembrance of Him who bore our sins on the Cross, whose sinless body was broken and whose atoning blood was shed so that those who believe might not perish but, instead, might live forever with God. Another strand of original Methodism was tough discipline, intended to strengthen the Body of Christ, to protect the weak and rehabilitate the backslider. Another strand was commonsense organization in a connectional system of church government under the Headship of Christ. Another was insatiable desire for knowledge, reason and wisdom—under governance of the Holy Spirit. Another was the compulsion for doing good, especially to those within the household of faith.

These and other Wesleyan strands entwined to form the mighty rope known as original Methodism. But ever since the beginning, Methodists have had the bad habit of taking one or two strands and insisting *"This* is Methodism!" For example, in America, conversion quickly came to dominate and eclipse other Methodist strands. The number of sinners at the altar became the be-all, end-all of Methodist success. One casualty of revivalism was Holy Communion. Along the American frontier there were not enough ordained Methodist ministers to serve the sacrament often. So it was usually skipped in favor of preaching, testimony, exhortation, and prayer.

The insignificance of Holy Communion is one hallmark of American Methodism today. This is an obvious sign of drastic departure from the original Methodism of the Wesleys and, of course, from the New Testament.

Another great deviation needs noting: Methodism became a mirror of American culture. This can be seen in sectional divisions about slavery, lasting from 1845 to 1939. But above all, culture conformity is revealed by the Methodist mania for statistical success—exemplified by big buildings, budgets, and membership rolls. Long ago, Methodism became the Great American Religion, an accepted part of our culture along with the Shrine and the Rotary Club. But original Methodism was so radically different from the prevailing English culture that early Methodists were often ridiculed and persecuted as dangerous fanatics. Their motto was not "the world sets our agenda" but "do not conform outwardly to the standards of this world, but let God transform you inwardly by a complete change of your mind. Then you will be able to know the will of God—what is good, and is pleasing to him, and is perfect" (Romans 12: 2, TEV).

American Methodism—in its various branches—is a mutation of the Wesleyan original. That is why this book says little about Methodism in the New World. The following pages seek to explore the basic Wesleyan doctrines, which reveal the anatomy of Wesleyan faith—one of the most phenomenal religious movements in world history.

Far from being a musty relic of the eighteenth century, original Methodism is a radical and largely unmet challenge to follow and obey Jesus Christ. The Wesleys are not behind us but ahead of us—far ahead! They challenge us to unexplored dimensions of personal sacrifice, discipline and practical love for the God who has loved us eternally in Christ.

CHARLES W. KEYSOR
Wilmore, Kentucky

Foreword

As I write these introductory words the United Methodist ministers of the Dakotas are meeting for their Pastors' School. The theme is "Unity in Diversity." They are hearing papers on pentecostalism and social activism, on the Good News movement within their church and on Chicago's Ecumenical Institute. The two main resource persons are one of the nation's outstanding Gospel preachers and one of our most able leaders of encounter groups. The school was designed to help us appreciate the validity of differences within our ranks. Few things are more important today.

In the new *United Methodist Primer* I wrote:

"Because of the diversity of its membership there is no such thing as a 'Methodist' point of view . . . Wesley once said, 'A string of opinions is no more Christian faith than a string of beads is Christian holiness.' People, not opinions, are at the heart of our response to human need. Jesus did not give his followers any sort of an ideological test before they became disciples. He simply said, 'Follow me.' He did not make it easy for them; his was not the way of 'cheap grace.' He said, 'If anyone will come after me let him deny himself, take up his cross daily, and follow . . .' (Luke 9: 23). But, he did not force a set of beliefs on anyone. He insisted on total commitment, not total agreement . . . We are called to tolerate, to live with, yes, to rejoice in our differences, all the while professing and demonstrating our oneness in Christ."

Charles W. Keysor, editor of *Good News* magazine and one of the key figures in the evangelical "caucus" of the United Methodist Church, has written this slim volume. It reflects a point of view consistent with our eighteenth century heritage. It will be deeply appreciated by many who are waiting for a heart-warming, soul-searching word about the grace offered freely in Jesus Christ; a grace that can literally fashion us into "new creatures." Others will write with more academic sophistication and an appreciative awareness of contemporary theological trends. Others will give more space to the relationship of the Wesleyan witness to constructive social change. Critics will raise questions about some of the author's interpretations of Biblical truth, the evolution of John Wesley, problems facing the church in today's world and his view of "last things." This is as it should be, for out of continuing dialogue comes further understanding and growth in grace.

In the meantime, I thank God for Charles Keysor and the Good News Movement within my denomination. They are reminding us of the authority of Scripture and personal religious experience. There is no "whole gospel" apart from these emphases. To the degree that we trust one another, honor principles of fair play and deal with the truth accurately and consistently, God can and will use us in doing His will. And ultimately—in all things— He will be the judge.

JAMES ARMSTRONG
Resident Bishop, Dakotas Area
United Methodist Church

1

You Are Seeking God

WHAT IS A METHODIST? Ask six people and you may get six different answers.

But the original Methodist, John Wesley, had no doubt. In a pamphlet called *Character of a Methodist,* he said that a Methodist is a person whose faith and life are what the Bible says faith and life ought to be.

The Bible says a lot about people searching to find God. Abel was seeking the Lord when he sacrificed in ancient times. Abraham the Hebrew patriarch was seeking God when he left his home city of Ur. He went hunting for a city whose builder is the living God (Hebrews 11: 10). Another seeker was John the Baptist, last of the Old Testament prophets. He kept looking for Christ: God come to walk and talk among ordinary people.

The list of God-searchers goes on and on. Paul . . . Augustine . . . Francis of Assisi . . . Savonarola . . . Martin Luther . . . Calvin . . . Wesley . . . Otterbein . . . Asbury . . . Finney . . . Moody . . . Kagawa . . . Rauschenbush . . . E. Stanley Jones . . . George Washington Carver . . . Henry Clay Morrison . . . Sundar Singh . . . Dietrich Bonhoeffer . . . J. C. McPheeters . . . you . . . me.

Seeking God is one of the deepest and most basic human quests: "Thou hast made us for Thyself," observed Augustine, a fifth-century theologian, "and we are restless until we find our rest in Thee."

Here is where the life of John Wesley touches us. He was a man who searched desperately for God. Once he really met God, the thirty-five-year-old Anglican priest embarked on the believer's search to know and serve better the God who had warmed his heart at Aldersgate and who touched him the same night with Holy Spirit fire. Through Wesley's two-fold search, God kindled one of the mightiest religious movements in history. Spreading from the burning heart of John Wesley, life-changing Methodist faith in Jesus Christ circled the globe, brought millions of people into God's Kingdom and put the impress of Christ upon world history.

Some important principles can be seen as we look at the first Methodist's search for God.

Principle One: *Sometimes it is hard to find God if you have grown up in the church.* John Wesley was born June 28, 1703, the fifteenth child of the Reverend Samuel Wesley and his wife Susanna. Samuel was a priest of England's official denomination, the Anglican Church. So John drew his first breath in the Epworth parsonage (known as "rectory"). There was no public school for children in those days, so John's mother was teacher for the Wesley family. How to pray was one of the earliest lessons. Each child was taught the alphabet on his or her fifth birthday. Of course the Bible was the Wesleys' primary reader. John Wesley learned Hebrew and Greek, so he was able to read the Bible in the original languages. He studied theology in college, then was ordained a priest. He preached. He baptized infants. He said thousands of formal prayers. He

14

served Holy Communion.

Nobody grew up inside the church more than John Wesley. But he did not really find God until his thirty-fifth year.

Principle Two: *The searcher stumbles into many blind alleys.* Like many others before and since, Wesley thought he was a Christian because he had godly parents; because he belonged to the church and did what the church prescribed. These things were helpful in preparing Wesley to be converted. But his faith remained like a light not plugged in until he realized that Christ's death upon the Cross had been for him, until he realized that Jesus' atoning death on Calvary had cancelled out his sins and made him fully a child of God (Galatians 3: 26). Only then did John Wesley escape from the blind alley of vague, general religion, which had the form of true godliness, but none of God's power (II Timothy 3: 5). Only after God had touched him personally did John Wesley have the faith he had searched for so intensely. With it came the vital power of God. For now in Christ, Wesley was connected to the supreme source of wisdom, strength, joy, peace, and righteousness.

Another of John Wesley's blind alleys was thinking that by doing many good works he could fulfill God's requirements. At Christ Church College, Oxford, John and his younger brother, Charles, established what came to be known as "the Holy Club." Jeering college students scoffed at these "Methodists" who tried systematically to serve God every hour of the day. They set aside time for praying. For examining their spiritual lives. For studying the Bible. For meeting together. For taking food to poor families, visiting lonely people in jail, teaching orphans to read. Critics on the Oxford campus said:

> By rule they eat, by rule they drink,
> By rule do all things but think.
> Accuse the priests of loose behavior

  To get more in the laymen's favor.
Method alone must guide 'em all
  When themselves "Methodists" they call.

After he had found God, Wesley looked back on these Oxford days and reflected that he had been a good Pharisee. His was the all-too-familiar disease: "I'll make myself good enough." This failed to bring real satisfaction to John Wesley—and to multitudes today who are, like Wesley was, in bondage . . . empty and barren of soul, in spite of all their church work.

Another blind alley for John Wesley was missionary service. On October 14, 1735, John and Charles Wesley sailed to America to work in the infant colony of Georgia. John returned to England in 1738 even more frustrated.

"My chief motive is the hope of saving my own soul," he wrote in his journal, just before leaving England.

But the missionary journey had important consequences: Wesley met some people who showed the kind of faith he wanted. Sailing to America on board the 250-ton ship, Simmonds, there was a frightful storm. Huge, green Atlantic waves heaved and tossed the frail ship. The gale roared and each moment seemed like the last. The mainsail split "with a noise like thunder" and terror gripped John Wesley. His formal prayers, his obsessive discipline, his endless rituals were powerless before the specter of death. Then Wesley saw an amazing sight: a group of Germans, singing psalms, rejoicing and giving thanks to God! Afterward he asked one German, "Weren't you afraid?"

"I thank God, no."

"But weren't your women and children afraid?"

"No, they are not afraid to die."

How the English priest admired and desired this perfect love of God which casts out fear (I John 4: 18)!

Principle Three: *In moments of extremity, when self-sufficiency has been punctured and the soul stands naked in weakness, God sends His witnesses.* In Wesley's case it was the Moravians. In America he met a Moravian missionary named Augustus Spangenberg. The diary of Wesley shows how God used this man to bring John Wesley one step closer to the Father's house.

Spangenberg: "Does the Spirit of God bear witness with your spirit that you are a child of God?"

Wesley was surprised and didn't know what to answer.

Spangenberg: "Do you know Jesus Christ?"

Wesley: "I know Him to be the Savior of the world."

Spangenberg: "True, but do you know that He has saved you?"

Wesley: "I hope He has died for me."

Spangenberg continued pressing and John Wesley dodged and wriggled—pretending mightily to cover the inner alarm which deepened as he realized his lack of faith.

By now John Wesley was approaching the dangerous age of thirty-five. This is the time when many men realize that their early dreams are dead or dying. When a man looks wistfully backward over the spent years and says to himself, "Half of my life is gone. What does it all amount to?" When a man peers apprehensively into the unknown future and wonders, "Will the rest of my life be so empty?"

This middle-age miasma was upon John Wesley as he came back to England in early 1738. His missionary service in Georgia had been a dismal failure. Rigid emphasis upon rules, rules, rules angered and repulsed most colonists. They hated or ignored the conscientious priest who insisted on reading morning and evening prayers, who arbitrarily excluded people from the Lord's Supper, and who baptized babies by immersion.

Would John Wesley never find himself? Would he go through life a highly educated misfit? Such wonderings pulled John Wesley deeper into what has been described as the "dark night of the soul." And it was darkest just before the dawn.

Principle Four: *God in His great and perfect wisdom, knows it is necessary for a person's self-reliance to be broken before full trust and dependence can be placed upon God alone.*

Back in England, Wesley met another Moravian pastor, Peter Boehler. He spent a lot of time with the Wesley brothers. In love he saw them as wretched, empty seekers after the living God, preaching a mixture of philosophy and religion-in-general.

"My brother," Boehler said to John Wesley, "that philosophy of yours must be purged away."

What, then, was Wesley supposed to preach?

"Preach faith until you have it," Boehler advised. "Then, because you have it, you will preach faith."

About this time Boehler introduced the Wesleys to some Moravians who gave personal testimonies that Christ was dwelling in them—and to the inner peace which He brings. The Wesley brothers could not argue against such evidence, and on March 5, 1778, Wesley wept bitter tears and confessed, "I was clearly convinced of my unbelief, of the want of faith whereby alone we are saved."

Englishmen were fascinated by America. So when Wesley went to preach in a church, crowds came to hear a firsthand report from the New World. What a surprise they got! Instead, Wesley preached that their comfortable, in-a-rut religion was not Christianity, or at best half Christian. Wesley told shocked congregations that the Lord required more of them than baptism, attending the sacraments—in short, more than being a good "churchman."

"You must be born again!" Wesley declared, borrowing the very words of Jesus (John 3: 3, 5, 7). Pure love for God and neighbor is what matters to God. To have such love, all need to be converted—good laymen and even ministers.

To complacent churchmen, this Bible message was like pouring gasoline on a fire—they exploded. Outraged priests forbade John Wesley to preach any more in their pulpits.

Principle Five: *Searching for God often leads you into hostility and misunderstanding.* As John Wesley drew closer to God he was, automatically, drawing farther and farther away from those who were content to remain as he had been: "separated from Christ, alienated from the commonwealth of Israel [God's People], and strangers to the covenants of promise, having no hope and without God in the world" (Ephesians 2: 12, RSV).

The Bible clearly teaches that basic hostility exists between redeemed people and those not redeemed. They live in two different kingdoms—one ruled by God and the other by Satan. To expect the world to approve and applaud godliness is a false hope. In fact, Scripture makes it clear that if you are a friend of God you will draw down upon yourself the hostility of those who do not know God (James 4: 4 and John 15: 18).

Principle Six: *"Draw nigh to God, and he will draw nigh to you"* (James 4: 8).

Stumbling, groping, failing, falling, torn and bruised of spirit, John Wesley moved closer to God. And God took a step toward John Wesley each time the seeker stepped toward Him. On May 24, 1738, someone invited him to attend a Bible study group led by a layman. Wesley went "unwillingly," according to his journal.

Sitting at the feet of a layman—the ultimate symbol of humiliation for a high churchman—John Wesley made the final step in his long, painful journey to God. Listen to the words with which the original Methodist describes it:

"While he [layman reading Luther] was describing the change which God works in the heart through faith in Christ, I felt my heart strangely warmed. I felt I did trust Christ, Christ alone, for salvation; and an assurance was given me that He had taken away my sins, even mine, and saved me from the law of sin and death. I began to pray with all my might for those who had . . . despitefully used me and persecuted me. . . ."

Principle Seven: *God sometimes uses unlikely situations and people as stepping-stones to Him.* In this case, God used a layman to finally lead John Wesley out of slavery and defeat into His marvelous grace. This miracle happened not in an austerely beautiful church but in a plain room surrounded by ordinary Christians—probably all laymen.

Principle Eight: *God used the Scriptures (Martin Luther's commentary on Romans) to make the final breakthrough.* The Bible is God's special lasso for drawing people to Himself. Therefore the Bible is at the center of any successful search for the living God. Without the Bible to establish what is God's truth, popular religion often blocks a person's way to God. In Wesley's case, this spiritual blockade was a familiar teaching of popular religion: save yourself by your own efforts. The Bible clearly lays to rest this false idea: "For by grace [the undeserved kindness of God] are ye saved through faith; and that not of yourselves: it is the gift of God: Not of works, lest any man should boast" (Ephesians 2: 8, 9).

Principle Nine: *Wesley did not experience God until he trusted Jesus Christ alone for salvation.* Christ became the center of his faith and redemption, fulfilling Jesus' own words, "No man cometh unto the Father, but by me" (John 14: 6b).

History shows the tendency, in every age, for the church to forget Jesus—to put Him in second, third, or last place. Whenever this happens the church becomes anemic and people fail to find God within the church. God is met where people encounter Jesus Christ, the God-Man. This may happen in a church service, a prayer group or a Bible study in someone's living room.

Principle Ten: *John Wesley's long search for God was rewarded among God's people.*

God works miracles "where two or three are gathered together in my [Christ's] name" (Matthew 18: 20). Where Jesus is, there is always power, love overflowing and miracles as a sign of His supreme greatness.

Principle Eleven: *At conversion, God immediately changed John Wesley's relationship to other people.* The first recorded result of his new personal relationship with God was awareness that his sins were forgiven as he trusted in Christ alone for deliverance. Next, Wesley began praying for people who had wronged him.

When you really find God, you also find a new, more Christlike relationship to other people (I John 3: 11-18; 4: 7-12, 19-21). After the Aldersgate meeting John Wesley went rushing over to see his younger brother. (Just three days earlier, Charles had found God. Soon afterward he wrote a hymn, a characteristic response of Charles Wesley, who eventually authored more than 6,000 hymns.) It was a preview of great things to come when John and Charles, meeting for the first time as "brothers in Christ," sang together,

> Where shall my wondering soul begin?
>   How shall I all to Heaven aspire?
> A slave redeemed from death and sin,
>   A brand plucked from eternal fire.

The story of John Wesley's search for God does not end here. Aldersgate is only the opening chapter. Now, the character of the search changes. It is like a road that gets wider and wider as you travel down it. After your glorious first meeting with God, then your Father-child relationship with Him should grow deeper and richer, much as married love ideally grows from honeymoon to golden wedding anniversary.

It is God's plan for this precious relationship to continue forever. But Methodists have always realized that God does allow converted persons freedom to turn away from Him. Methodists call this "falling from grace," or "backsliding." It is clearly taught in II Peter 2: 20-22; Galatians 4: 8, 9; 5: 4; Hebrews 6: 4. God does not take away from you the same dangerous freedom which Adam misused when he disobeyed God (Genesis 3). As the Russian philosopher Nikolai Berdyaev has said, "If a man is not free to go to hell, he is not really free."

The journal of John Wesley is an honest record of this great Christian's ups and downs over many years. It shows us that after he first trusted Christ at Aldersgate, the search for a closer relationship with God went on and on. A final glimpse is permitted to us. In 1791, John Wesley, age 88, lies on his deathbed. Behind him is a record of some 400,000 sermons, $150,000 given to charitable causes, countless people converted and a great religious movement known as Methodism stretching its influence to other continents. His strength ebbing, Wesley sings feebly a favorite hymn:

> I'll praise my Maker while I've breath:
> And when my voice is lost in death,
> Praise shall employ my nobler powers:
> My days of praise shall ne'er be past,
> While life, and thought, and being last,
> Or immortality endures.

His dying words: "Best of all, God is with us."

QUESTIONS FOR DISCUSSION

1. *Is it necessary for everybody to have an "Aldersgate experience" like John Wesley?*

2. *What similarities can you see between John Wesley's search for God and yours?*

3. *What is the end of a person's search for God?*

4. *What place should Jesus Christ occupy in our search for God? Do people find God without Christ being involved? Explain.*

5. Do you think there are very many people who grow up inside the church without really "finding" God? What can a church do to make sure people find God in and through the church?

6. What people did God use to help John Wesley come to Him? What people helped you discover God?

7. If God loves people, why does He allow them to struggle and suffer before they find Him?

8. It has been said that Christianity is not a matter of man seeking God, but of God seeking man. Do you agree? How would you relate this to the story of John Wesley, as told in chapter one?

9. John Wesley made several mistakes in trying to find God. These were described as "blind alleys." Can you remember them? Do you know of anybody who has made the same mistakes?

10. Is it possible to do many good works and still not be a Christian? Why? Is it possible to be a real Christian and not do good works?

11. It has been said that John Wesley's experience at Aldersgate established a dramatic conversion emphasis among generations of Methodists. Can one person's experience set the "norm" for others? Why or why not?

12. What place did the Body of Christ—the community of believers—play in John Wesley's search for God? Can a person find God outside the church? Explain your answers.

2

You Do Good to Everyone

IT WAS ONE OF THOSE "social action" Methodist churches.

First, there was a school for poor children, operated eleven hours daily.

The church was the site of a "house of mercy" where board and room was given to destitute widows, unwanted orphans, and blind people.

A dispensary also operated out of the church, offering the free services of a pharmacist and surgeon to some 100 needy people every month.

Another phase of the church social program was a savings bank. Church members could deposit their money, knowing it would be used to help poverty-stricken families facing financial crisis. It was a kind of credit union.

In the church was a thriving bookstore.

This socially conscious Methodist church was also a place of worship. Hundreds of people came on Sunday and during the week to hear the Gospel preached, to sing God's praises, to pray, to study the Bible, and to fellowship with other Christians.

Last but not least, the church provided living quarters for a traveling preacher named John Wesley. Between itinerant preaching missions he lived in this church—as did his aging mother. It was the world's first Methodist church, established by John Wesley himself.

This church was not a freak. It simply reflected the top-to-bottom social concern which was woven into original Methodism's very soul and being. This is why the influential London Spectator wrote:

"The Roman church has been called the church of the poor; but that title of honor belongs quite as much, if not with a better right, to the Wesleyan body."

Jacob Riis was a Danish journalist who came to the United States in 1870. Working as a reporter in New York City, Riis, a Methodist, became one of America's leading social reformers. He wrote:

"Methodism girdles the globe. It does definitely more than that. It lies close to the heart of mankind."

All of this may sound strange in a day when Methodists are accustomed to an either-or split between Christians who think in terms of social concerns and others who think mostly in terms of praying, preaching, and converting lost sinners. This dichotomy—this split Christian personality—was not known to John Wesley. He was a Bible Christian, and following the Bible led him to embrace both sides of the social vs. spiritual argument.

The present un-Biblical split between these two authentic parts of the Gospel is one of the most radical departures from original Methodism. For John Wesley regarded them both as necessary ingredients of "Scriptural holiness" and "Scriptural Christianity." But Methodism in our time has divided them into two warring camps. It is as if mainline Methodists have developed religious schizophrenia—a split into two personalities.

One of these can broadly be called "spiritual." It was

and is characterized by camp meetings, revivals, foreign missionary concern, and eager pursuit of religious experience. Its outward manifestation was the founding of many new churches and adding many people to the church membership rolls. This was the dominant viewpoint in mainline Methodism until the closing decades of the nineteenth century. It produced many "good works," in truly Methodist fashion: efforts to liberate enslaved blacks; establishing schools, orphanages, and hospitals across the continent; combatting the evils of alcohol; sending missionaries around the world. These good works were seen as the necessary sequel to conversion—and thus were squarely in line with John Wesley's goal for Methodists as leaven for God working in the world.

However, there was a blindness to many social needs and problems. Indeed, Methodists often became perpetrators of, or passive assenters to, injustice. Charles Furgeson said in his book, *Organizing to Beat the Devil,* that Methodism in the nineteenth century became the perfect mirror and reflection of American culture. Thus Methodism lost much of its tension with the established culture, in direct violation of its Biblical, Wesleyan heritage —"Do not conform outwardly to the standards of this world, but let God transform you inwardly by a complete change of your mind" (Romans 12: 2, TEV).

The widespread Victorian Methodist indignation over the evils of alcohol was not matched by equal indignation over white men (including Methodists) stealing a whole continent from red men. Enthusiasm for freeing slaves was not matched, after abolition, by continuing zeal to help the former slaves adjust to their new freedom. Methodist indignation against sin-in-general did not seem to include much indignation over the rape of America's natural resources by the robber barons of laissez faire capitalism. And the growing complexity of national life, brought about by enlarging cities and the rapid growth of industry, seemed outside the concern of the Methodist mainstream.

These blind spots led to a movement to counteract them—to relate the Christian faith more specifically to America's increasingly complex economic and social life. Thus was born the second of Methodism's split personalities, the so-called "social Gospel." Methodist Jacob Riis and Baptist Walter Rauschenbush, along with many others, rapidly pulled the church in this direction. Their followers merged and mingled with a tide of philosophy, theology, and Biblical criticism coming from Europe. Together these captured Methodism's seminaries and colleges, where future church leaders were being trained. Thus the Methodist elite—future bishops, preachers, and bureaucrats—turned away from the Methodist traditionalism. The differences of viewpoint climaxed in the Modernist-Fundamentalist controversy of the 1920s, ended with a total victory by the "liberals." This was the climax of a forty-year revolution which turned mainline Methodism in a different direction. This mood and spirit continue to the present day. But even as a speeding bullet curves away from its original target, falling, spent, to the ground, so the social passion of Riis and Rauschenbush changed course and lost momentum. During the 1930s and 40s Methodist social concern focused on world peace and the consequences of social upheaval caused by the Great Depression. World War II killed off Methodist pacifism until it resurfaced in the 1960s as opposition to the Vietnam war.

After World War II the zeal of the original social Gospel hardened into liberal institutionalism. Its exponents had become old men resistant to change as had been their traditionalist opponents of the previous generation.

Growth of the church bureaucracy through the twentieth century led to formation of power blocs within the church. The earliest of these were the Boards of Social

Concern, Missions and Education. These were headed by professional church bureaucrats who wielded increasing power and influence. Then, in the late 1960s, so-called caucuses emerged to complete and make visible the politicizing of Methodism. Methodists and Black Methodists for Church Renewal were the most effective. Other caucuses developed in the early 1970s: women's rights, homosexuality, seminarians, Spanish-speaking Americans, Orientals, and Indians. (On the conservative side, the Good News Movement began in 1966, but it was not like the others because it did not seek denominational power and money.)

In a fragmented way these special interest groups carried forward the classic Methodist ideal of doing good.

But even as Methodist compassion was being thus politicized and specialized, a new enemy appeared. Its name was institutionalism: the putting first of the church as an institution. Of course this was nothing new. But it suddenly grew dominant after the mainline Methodism's brief flirtation with the political "new left" in the late 1960s. The triumph of institutionalism was revealed by the 1972 United Methodist General Conference, which spent most of its time and energy overhauling the church bureaucracy. The Wesleyan passion for meeting human need—both physical and spiritual—was eclipsed. In its place emerged organization charts and a quietly deepening emphasis on conformity to denominational thinking, in spite of much-advertised "pluralism." The religious organization man now controls mainline Methodism. Unwelcome is the prophet who thunders that God's justice will roll down like a mighty stream upon a church and a society characterized by violence and injustice. Unwelcome, too, is the other sort of prophet who declares in the words of Jesus, "You must all be born again" (John 3: 7, TEV).

Here we stand. It seems a long, long way back to that

compassionate first Methodist church which John Wesley established. But is it really "back"? Instead, is it not forward? Was not the original Methodist far ahead of us in comprehending the will of God and the nature of Christian faith as "close to the heart of mankind"?

To follow John Wesley would lead Methodism into new frontiers of perfect love. To follow him is to follow the One whom Wesley supremely loved and sought to obey, the Lord Jesus Christ. He was vitally concerned about the whole person's welfare in this world and in the next.

Modern Methodists ought to read John Wesley's Journal for January 4-9, 1785. He was 82 years old, and this is what happened:

"On this and the four following days I walked through the town and begged two hundred pounds (one thousand dollars) in order to clothe them that needed it most. But it was hard work, as most of the streets were filled with melting snow, which often lay ankle-deep, so that my feet were steeped in snow water nearly from morning till evening. I held out pretty well till Saturday evening, but I was laid up with a violent flux . . .

"This increased every hour till, at six in the morning, Dr. Whitehead called upon me. His first draught made me quite easy, and three or four more perfected the cure. If he lives some years, I expect he will be one of the most eminent physicians in Europe."

How can this sort of compassion be restored? The whole church—including individual members, programs, and hierarchy—needs new birth. Nothing else can make us like the 82-year-old man who trudged through the snow four days to collect money to buy clothes for the poor. Being born again makes people fools for Christ. And this is one thing it means to be a Methodist.

QUESTIONS FOR DISCUSSION
1. *How would you like to belong to the original Meth-*

29

odist Church, described at the beginning of this chapter? In what ways does it sound like your own church? In what ways different?

2. What makes a church "close to the heart of mankind"?

3. What has caused the splitting of one Gospel into a "social Gospel" and what might be called a "spiritual Gospel"? Was this split evident in the Methodism of John Wesley?

4. Would you agree that a great and monstrous heresy exists when the church stops caring for people?

5. What caused 82-year-old John Wesley to endure hardship collecting money to clothe needy people? Do you think he would have been better serving Christ if he had spent his time preaching or working out the problems of the many Methodist societies? What Scripture can you find to support your opinion?

6. Does the term "do-gooder" suggest a certain scorn? Do some people really look down upon others who do good?

7. Is it possible to care whether a person is lost or saved without also caring if he or she is hungry, lives in a substandard house, sends children to a poor school, cannot get equal pay because of discrimination? Did Jesus minister strictly to the soul or to the body or both? Give some examples from the Bible.

8. Can a church building be a hindrance to a congregation in following Christ? Explain your answer.

9. Read Matthew 25: 31-46. What does this say about the importance of "doing good to everyone"? Does it mean that people are saved as a result of their good works?

10. How can a person develop genuine love and concern for other people? Does this come through education, right upbringing, association with the church, or what?

11. Think of the church you know best. Does it have the kind of social outreach practiced by Wesley's original Methodist congregation, described at the start of this chapter? Why or why not?

12. What was the connection between Methodism's historic emphasis on conversion and the doing of good works? What happens to good works when the conversion emphasis is forgotten? To conversion when good works are forgotten?

3

You Are a Jesus Person

SOMETIME DURING THE 1960s, when America was boiling with revolutions too numerous to mention, a different sort of American revolution got under way. It started among young people—teens and young adults, especially those in the dropout and drug scene, known also as "counterculture."

This was a religious revolution, more specifically a "Jesus Revolution." The Person of Jesus Christ was its heart and center. In this movement were youth who had quit established churches, who had been tripping on everything from LSD to satanism and communal sex. Out of this improbable background, multitudes became fascinated by Jesus. In the Man of Galilee they found one who could identify with them in their feelings of emptiness and revulsion from the artificiality of postwar American life, identified as the "plastic culture."

As they turned to Jesus, He lifted them out of despair into ecstasy. He worked miracles, releasing captives from slavery to drugs; restoring ultimate meaning to lives which lacked meaning; giving a sense of cohesion and divine purpose to those for whom life had, before Christ, seemed a monstrous absurdity with "no exit."

To many of these—the social outcasts of modern America—Jesus became Savior. Lord. They began living in Jesus communes, seeking to create "life together" after the New Testament ideal. In the name and Spirit of Jesus they loved and helped drug addicts and runaways who were alienated from their parents. They were joyously baptized in the name of Jesus; they learned to pray fervently through Him and to Him. They talked constantly about Him—among themselves, and to strangers on the streets. They printed millions of newspapers, tracts, and posters. They showed Jesus as the strong, love-filled revolutionary rather than the namby-pamby, effeminate ascetic, an image blasphemously perpetuated in the art of traditional American religion (which the youth had long ago rejected as loveless, joyless, and powerless). Jesus buttons and bumper stickers were seen everywhere. "Honk if you love Jesus" was a favorite.

The universal symbol of the Jesus Revolution is the hand upraised with index finger pointed upward symbolizing Jesus as the one way for mankind. Jesus Himself said, "I am the way, and the truth, and the life; no one comes to the Father, but by me" (John 14: 6). Because they believed this literally, they began to live accordingly. These were true revolutionaries, feared, mocked, and despised by religious traditionalists who could not see beyond their long hair and freaky clothes. Jesus was their only Savior, best friend, miracle deliverer, and constant companion.

This Jesus Revolution runs contrary to the religious emphasis in many churches where, over a period of years, Jesus has been gradually eclipsed or so distorted from Biblical reality that He has been fitted comfortably into

32

the church routine. Biblical criticism, which arrived from Europe, beginning in the 1880s, had the effect of stripping away Jesus' deity and emphasizing Jesus the man. Jesus-minus-deity was no longer necessary for He was nothing more than a great man. Without being God He could not be Lord of the church or of people's lives.

The eclipse of Jesus cast a paralysis across the faith of mainline Methodism. Jesus, whom God appointed to be the head of the church, became little more than a toe. Before Him came building programs, church suppers, circle meetings, men's clubs, bazaars, business meetings, study books on secular topics, and "fellowship" at which church members happily watched movies about auto racing or listened to speakers showing ladies how to make fancy hats. A thousand matters of "churchmanship" pushed Jesus further and further into the background—even though He can still be seen impersonally enshrined in stained-glass windows—a safe place to keep this radical upsetter of the status quo!

It was not accidental that public interest in the church declined in exact proportion to the diminishing emphasis on Jesus Christ as Savior and Lord. Youth, especially, were excited by Jesus as they read about Him in the Bible. But they noticed His absence from the church, and this has been one major cause of youth's present lack of enthusiasm for institutional churches. A college student was talking on a Florida beach with a Christian worker. The student, speaking for many of her contemporaries, asked, "If I take Jesus do I have to take the church?"

The idea of a church without Jesus Christ as the head, the absolute center, and the source of all wisdom and power, is foreign to real Methodism. In his tract, *Character of a Methodist,* John Wesley wrote, "The Methodist trusts in Christ alone for his or her salvation. The Methodist knows that the blood of Jesus has cleansed him from all sin. Through Christ and Christ alone the Methodist has received forgiveness for his sins."

The Wesley hymns sung by Methodists even today are so interwoven with Jesus Christ that to remove Him would be like taking the foundation out from under a building.

Charles Wesley wrote, and generations of Methodists have sung with deep conviction:

> Jesus! the Name high over all
>   In hell or earth or sky
> Angels and men before it fall
>   And devils fear and fly.
>
> Jesus! the Name to sinners dear
>   The Name to sinners given
> It scatters all their guilty fear
>   It turns their hell to heaven,
>
> Happy if with my latest breath
>   I may but gasp His Name
> Preach Him to all, and cry in death
>   "Behold, behold the Lamb!"

Jesus is the very heart of Methodism—Christless, religion-in-general is no more Methodism than a jet airplane is a canoe. For this reason every real Methodist is, actually, a "Jesus Person." And historic Methodist faith is fixed solidly upon what theologians call a "high Christology." This is a technical term for the Bible's exalted teaching that Jesus Christ is ". . . the name which is above every name, that at the name of Jesus every knee should bow, in heaven and on earth and under the earth, and every tongue confess that Jesus Christ is Lord, to the glory of God the Father" (Philippians 2: 9b-11, RSV). It is no mere accident that the earliest Christian creed was probably, "Jesus is Lord!" (I Corinthians 12: 3). On Him was built the church, the faith, everything (I Corinthians 3: 11).

This Biblical note of Jesus' absolute supremacy (Lordship) is woven through the hymns and writings of the

Wesleys, forever and unalterably linking the heart of Methodism and Methodists with the person of the Son of God. To the extent that a Methodist or a church departs from this evident centrality of Jesus Christ, that person or church has strayed away from its heritage of Methodist Bible Christianity.

No human mind can fully understand Jesus Christ. Who can claim to know the full meaning of who He is, what He has done, and what He will do finally "when the roll is called up yonder and time will be no more"? But believers are instructed to "run with perseverance the race that is set before us, looking to Jesus the pioneer and perfecter of our faith" (Hebrews 12: 1b, 2a).

As Christians seeking to understand the Methodist way of Scriptural Christianity, we need to look deeply into the profound mystery of Jesus Christ, "that I may know him and the power of his resurrection" (Philippians 3: 10a).

Much is revealed about the mystery of Christ in the "hymn to Christ" included in the first chapter of Paul's letter to the Colossians. Here the Holy Spirit gave to Paul —and through his inspired pen gives to us—a summary of Bible teaching about the one "who gave himself for our sins to deliver us from the present evil age, according to the will of our God and Father; to whom be the glory for ever and ever. Amen" (Galatians 1: 4, 5).

In the following paragraphs, quoted sentences and phrases are from the key passage, Colossians 1: 15-20, RSV, followed by highlight explanations. These brief comments are intended only to suggest the majesty and mystery of our Savior.

"He [Christ] is the image of the invisible God" (vs. 15a): The Heavenly Father has showed (revealed) Himself to us in the person of Jesus, the Christ. To discover what God is like we must look at Jesus Christ who is the incarnation (enfleshment) of God. You can get partial knowledge about God from seeing His handiwork in na-

35

ture. But no real understanding of God is possible apart from knowing Jesus personally, from studying how He relates to people, from allowing His Spirit to energize His words from the Bible and to apply them directly and personally to your life. Jesus on the Cross shows that God loves even those who reject Him. Who can learn this from looking at a sunset or beautiful flower?

"[Christ is] the first-born of all creation" (vs. 15b): As God-come-to-Earth in the flesh, Jesus was the first representative of God's new and perfect humanity. By sending Jesus, God showed us an example of what people can and should be after they have been cleansed from sin and given a perfect love toward God and neighbor. If we are obedient to Jesus we shall become more and more like Him in this present life, possessing His very mind and walking even as He walked. Then, in death, we shall follow Jesus through the experience of dying and rising triumphant over death, hell, and the grave. Through Jesus Christ we are guaranteed a place close to God forever. Jesus was the first-born representative of the new and transformed humanity God intends for each and every person.

"For in him [Christ] all things were created, in heaven and on earth, visible and invisible, whether thrones or dominions or principalities or authorities—all things were created through him and for him" (vs. 16): Jesus has existed always. There never was a time when He was not. At a certain point in time He came to Earth at the manger in Bethlehem, but Jesus Christ was preexistent, that is, He has always been, coeternal with the Father and the Holy Spirit. In a way which nobody fully understands, Christ was actively engaged in the creation of the Earth. He continues to be the One through whom all things are created—each baby and each snowdrop, and each trembling soul who comes to God.

"He is before all things, and in him all things hold together" (vs. 17): Christ is the cohesive force holding together the whole vast realm of nature, all the way from the farthest star and galaxy to the minutest molecule. Organizations, family relationships, governments, everything, keep from falling apart only as Jesus Christ is acknowledged as God's cohesive, unifying force. When things do fall apart, it is because Christ is ignored and people try to make them cohere by their own wisdom, by science or by technology.

"He is the head of the body, the church" (vs. 18a): As the human body gets its direction from the head, so God intends for the church of Jesus Christ to depend utterly upon Jesus, its supreme Head. Apart from Him the church is just another organization—a headless corpse, not capable of pleasing God or making any constructive impact upon the world.

"He is the beginning, the first-born from the dead, that in everything he might be pre-eminent" (vs. 18b): God raised Jesus from the dead in order that Jesus might be "number one," preeminent in everything. First in all creation. First in holding the universe together. First example of the perfect man. First to atone (make payment by His sacrifice) for the sins of the world. First in the church. The source of its wisdom and power, the center of its witness, the controller of its correct faith and its proper behavior. When Jesus is preeminent in all things, then will be realized our familiar prayer, "Thy kingdom come, Thy will be done, On earth as it is in heaven."

"In him all the fulness of God was pleased to dwell, and through him to reconcile to himself all things, whether on earth or in heaven, making peace by the blood of his cross" (vs. 19, 20): The world is full of hostility. This is caused by sin, which came to curse the universe when the first man, Adam, disobeyed God. As a result, all people, all creatures, are in a wrong relationship with God, with each other and with themselves. Reconciliation is needed

—the bringing together of those who are separated, alienated, hostile, estranged.

This is why Jesus came to Earth, to make reconciliation possible. He accomplished this by dying on the Cross of Calvary. His suffering and sacrifice miraculously reconcile to God, others, and self, anyone who asks to be "reconciled to God by the death of his Son" (Romans 5: 10).

"He came for to die" is how a mountain folk song describes Jesus' mission. The Cross of Christ, therefore, is not tragedy but glory—the glory of God loving the world so much "that he gave his only Son, that whoever believes in him should not perish but have eternal life" (John 3: 16, RSV).

Believing all this about Jesus Christ, having personally met Jesus, having experienced a measure of the transforming power of His love, the true Methodist bows before the risen Jesus and says with Thomas, "My Lord and my God!" (John 20: 28).

> Christ, by highest Heaven adored,
> Christ the everlasting Lord
> Late in time behold Him come,
> Offspring of the virgin's womb!
>
> Veiled in flesh the Godhead see;
> Hail the Incarnate Deity!
> Pleased as man with men to dwell
> Jesus, or Immanuel.—*Charles Wesley*

QUESTIONS FOR DISCUSSION

1. *What does it mean that Jesus is the head of the church? Can you describe five things that might happen in your church if Jesus were really its head? Five things that might happen if somebody else were the church's head?*

2. *Do you agree that a church which ignores or minimizes Jesus Christ will have less attraction for youth? For adults? Why?*

3. *What are the reasons why a person might put something else ahead of Jesus as first priority?*

4. *What is meant by a "high Christology"? What is important about this?*

5. *Are you a "Jesus person"? Explain.*

6. *Many people say they find God in nature. Is this possible? How did God show us what He is really like?*

7. *Is it possible to "have Jesus" without also having the church?*

8. *Some people say that Christ is not necessary. How would you answer this? Could a Christian say this?*

9. *What would you say if someone asked you why Jesus is important?*

10. *What is it about Jesus that has attracted the attention of so many youth and young adults in the "Jesus Revolution"? What is it about Jesus that attracts you?*

11. *Where do people get their ideas of what Jesus is like? Is it possible, ever, for people to get a wrong picture of Jesus? How might this happen? How accurate is your idea of Jesus?*

12. *If the deity of Jesus Christ is removed, what effect would this have on the church? Is His deity important to you?*

4

You Offer Christ

OUT ON THE OCEAN BEACH, a Methodist and two college students huddle under a bright colored umbrella. They are looking at a little folder called "Four Spiritual Laws."

In one of the pits beside a drag strip, a long-haired Methodist is talking with several other young men. Their coveralls are smeared with oil and their conversation is sometimes drowned out by roaring motors on the nearby track. But the speaker has their attention. He is telling them about an exciting new life he has found in Jesus Christ.

Over cups of coffee in a kitchen, two middle-aged women are talking. One is facing a deep family problem. She pours out her trouble, her fears, and her doubts. Her friend, a Methodist, listens lovingly. And when her neighbor has "let it all hang out," the Methodist woman shares how Jesus has held her own family together through a major crisis.

It is Sunday morning. A Methodist congregation is listening to a sermon. The preacher is talking about national corruption, about the need for minority groups to be treated as persons, about migrant workers being exploited right in their own community. After cataloging the social problems, he takes a final step. The preacher identifies Jesus Christ as the one—the only one—who can put God's loving concern into the hearts of people who are indifferent to their neighbors.

Several Methodist laymen are out calling. They visit a home of parents who send their children to church school —but never bother to worship. The men show genuine personal interest in the family. They listen and learn what the man does for a living, where the children are in school. Easily, naturally, in the context of casual conversation, these visitors mention how important Jesus has become in their lives. They witness that He stands ready to work miracles in the lives of every family.

Evangelism has a thousand different faces. It has many different forms but always just one purpose—to tell about Jesus Christ, to testify to what He has done, is doing and will do, to point to Him as the center of all hope and meaning. Often John Wesley's journals report visiting in homes or preaching, and concludes with the phrase, "I offered them Christ."

For Methodists, this is a good description of evangelism. A practical working definition is much needed today, because there is great confusion about evangelism. Many people say that anything that churches or individual Christians do is evangelism. This word has come to mean just about everything from preaching, to church members working to desegregate public schools. Meaning everything, evangelism has often come to mean nothing.

What is evangelism?

The word comes from one root source: *evangel* (Good News of salvation). Webster's dictionary defines it as, "1: The message or news of man's redemption through

Christ; hence any of the four Gospels; 2: Good news; glad tidings." Evangelism, then, is the announcement of the Bible's glad tidings that salvation—wholeness—is now available in and through Jesus Christ.

Some current ideas of evangelism don't even mention Jesus or directly point people to Him. This is like taking water out of the ocean or heat from the fire. In the proper sense of the word—as Webster defined it and as Methodists since Wesley have understood it—true evangelism must feature Jesus Christ. Any sermon, teaching or action which does not clearly, directly and prominently offer Christ cannot properly be called evangelism in the Methodist tradition.

What does it mean to "offer Christ"?

The word "offer" means that one person gives and the other has the right to accept or reject. The responsibility of acceptance is upon the receiver—and he pays the consequences of saying yes or no to the offer. It means that you do not trick, wheedle, threaten or high-pressure. Instead, you make the truth of Christ inescapably clear. You offer it in the same way you offer directions to a stranger who stops in front of your house and asks, "How can I get to Smithville from here?"

You say, "Go down this road about two miles; then turn left at the first traffic signal."

Whether or not the stranger follows your directions is a matter for him to decide. You have given him accurate directions; the responsibility for following them rests with the other person. If he is wise he will take your directions and get to Smithville. But he is free to ignore your directions if he so chooses and get lost.

So it is with offering Christ. The responsibility of each Christian is first of all to know the basic facts of evangelism: who Jesus is, why He came to Earth, what He has done, what He promises to do for us, and, finally, what conditions must be met before His promises can become real in a person's life.

Much of today's weakness in evangelism is caused by church members' (and surprisingly, some pastors') having little or no idea of these basic Gospel facts.

Late one evening the custodian was closing up the church building after a meeting of the church board. Everyone had gone home and the custodian was there alone. Suddenly a stranger appeared.

"Can you help me?" he asked the custodian. "I've come to the end of my rope. I need to find God. I've been running away from Him a long time and tonight I decided to become a Christian. Please help me."

Suppose you had been this custodian. Would you have been able to guide this seeker into the Kingdom? Not without knowing the Gospel ABCs.

Who is Jesus? He is the Savior who came to introduce the world to the Heavenly Father. He is the *only way* by which people can make contact with the living God (John 14: 6). He is God in the flesh. He is the perfect man. Our teacher, example, and redeemer.

Why did Jesus come to Earth? His mission was to provide a bridge over which any person could return to God. He left Heaven to come to share every human suffering and humiliation. He came to prove that God loves us and wants to help us. "For God loved the world so much that he gave his only Son, so that everyone who believes in him may not die but have eternal life. For God did not send his Son into the world to be its Judge, but to be its Savior" (John 3: 16, 17, TEV).

What has Jesus done? First, Jesus has given us the teachings we need to become and remain Christians.

Second, He was crucified on the Cross, according to God's deliberate will and plan, in order to pay the penalty for the sins of anyone who believes in Him. This is called atonement. His death cancels out every past sin of every true believer, marking the record paid in full as far as

God is concerned. The death of Jesus automatically brings complete forgiveness to anyone who believes this—and proves belief sincere by obeying Jesus. Isaiah, chapter 53, describes this amazing miracle: "Yet it was *our* grief he bore, *our* sorrows that weighed him down. And we thought his troubles were a punishment from God, for his *own* sins! But he was wounded and bruised for *our* sins. He was chastised that we might have peace; he was lashed —and we were healed! *We* are the ones who strayed away like sheep! *We,* who left God's paths to follow our own. Yet God laid on *him* the guilt and sins of every one of us! . . . by the anguish of his soul, he shall be satisfied; and because of what he has experienced, my righteous Servant shall make many to be counted righteous before God, for he shall bear all their sins" (Isaiah 53: 4-6, 11, LB).

Third, after dying on the Cross of Calvary, Jesus was brought back to life on the third day. He rose out of the grave and He lives forever—confirming His promise that "I am the resurrection and the life; he who believes in me, though he die, yet shall he live, and whoever lives and believes in me shall never die" (John 11: 25, 26).

Jesus came to teach us, He died to save us from hell, and He rose to make real our confidence in the life everlasting . . . a life that begins when He becomes Savior.

What does Jesus promise? That if anyone invites Jesus into his or her life, He will come in (Revelation 3: 20). He will set us free from untruth (John 8: 31, 32). He will lead us into a life of abundance (John 10: 10), and joy (John 15: 11). Through inevitable suffering, He will make us victorious (I Cor. 15: 57). He will take away all guilt (II Cor. 5: 19) and give the "peace . . . which passeth all understanding" (Philippians 4: 7). He will create in us perfect love by which we can meet God's expectations (Romans 5: 15). Rest is promised (Mt. 11: 28). Likewise power to do mighty works for God (John 14: 12).

What conditions must be met before these promises can come true in a person's life? "I [Jesus] stand at the door and knock; if any one hears my voice and opens the door, I will come in to him and eat with him, and he with me" (Revelation 3: 20, RSV). "For man believes with his heart and so is justified, and he confesses with his lips and so is saved. The scripture says, 'No one who believes in him [Christ] will be put to shame' " (Romans 10: 10, 11, RSV).

To believe means simply to take God at His word. To trust that even those things we can't understand must be so if God has clearly promised them in the Bible. This is the faith of the all-trusting child, which Jesus explained is a necessity for all who would enter—and presumably continue in—God's Kingdom (Matthew 18: 3).

These basic Gospel facts must be grasped and believed before you "offer Christ." For without these great Bible principles as a foundation, a person may offer his or her own private ideas or experience and thus mislead hearers.

In his zeal for clean living, a misguided Christian says that anyone will go to hell if he smokes or drinks. Not so, according to the Bible. It says hell is for those who have not trusted Jesus as Savior (John 3: 16-18) and failed to obey His commandments as Lord (Matthew 25: 31-46). Some people think they are saved by abstaining from smoking and drinking, or by doing good deeds, or by going to church regularly, or by tithing. At the last Judgment, they will be startled to learn that a different standard will be enforced when the eternally saved are separated from the eternally damned. Great condemnation is in store for people who have wrongly led others to expect salvation on any grounds other than those clearly stated in the Bible.

The Holy Spirit leads a maturing Christian to abstain from anything harmful to self or others. But this is the result of salvation rather than the cause.

"Come to the altar and be saved," declares the fervent evangelist. But nobody can be saved simply by visiting an altar. It is coming to Christ which saves. Only this. If you find Christ at the altar and surrender to Him, then you will be saved—on the spot. But you can be saved at other places. In fact any place becomes an altar when a person turns genuinely to Jesus Christ. A bedroom. A commuter train. An airliner. Anywhere.

The evangelism of John Wesley reached around the world. It changed the lives of millions of people—who, in turn, profoundly affected their world. Wesley's evangelism amounted to clearly "offering Christ," trusting that Christ being lifted up would draw to Himself those who are ready to be saved. No tricks, no gimmicks. The pure offering of the all-powerful Son of God. Trust that He alone can save, that He desires to save all people, and that salvation is to be found in His name alone.

Another principle of Methodist evangelism is important. It can be understood through a modern parable.

Once there was a fisherman. He assembled all his equipment, got minnows and worms. Then he started fishing in his living room. He caught no fish, so he tried fishing in the garage. No luck there either.

"Why don't you go out to the lake?" his wife said. "There's where the fish are."

Obedient to his wife, the man went fishing in the lake —and got his limit of bass and bluegill.

How absurd to fish in the living room. How unthinkable that a fisherman should not go where the fish really are.

Jesus said to his disciples, "I will make you fishers of men" (Matthew 4: 19). To "catch" people for Christ, it is necessary to go where the people are.

In John Wesley's day, relatively few people came into the church buildings. So God sent John Wesley out to preach on crowded street corners, and at coal mine en-

46

trances where thousands of people stopped to listen. Wesley and the early Methodists brought the Good News of Jesus to the people; they didn't wait for the people to come to them.

In America, Methodist circuit riders ranged up and down the vast frontier. When the first settlers arrived, the Methodist preacher would soon be there. Other people built churches and waited for people to come to them; early Methodists went to the people, offering Christ. So it was that Methodists touched millions of lives with the Good News of Jesus Christ and Him crucified.

True Methodism is outreach. It is marked by restless creativity which does not rest content with old ways of evangelizing, but under Holy Spirit guidance, thrusts ever out to where the people are, offering them Jesus Christ.

The college-age Methodist mentioned at the start of this chapter moved out of the church building and offered Christ to his friends—where they were sunbathing and swimming.

The young Methodist minister at the dragstrip moved out of his pulpit. He was offering Christ where crowds of unchurched people gather at the dragstrip.

The middle-aged housewife did not drag her neighbor off to church, but offered Christ over coffee cups right in her own kitchen.

The preacher had a captive audience on Sunday morning. But he did not miss the opportunity to offer them Christ in the sanctuary. He did not assume that just because they had come to church they had no need of such an offer.

The laymen mentioned at the start of this chapter did not sit back and say, "we will offer Christ as soon as those neighbors come to church." Instead, they took the initiative. They went to the home of the nonchurchgoer and offered Christ right where they were.

A final principle of true Methodist evangelism: Every Christian is under sacred obligation to "offer Christ." Not only professional evangelists and ordained ministers. One reason for the death of evangelism in many churches has been the un-Biblical idea that evangelism is work for professionals only. Many laymen say, "Who, *me* offer Christ? That's the minister's job. That's what we have evangelists for. Don't ask *me* to witness. I'm only a layman."

The church has permitted—no, encouraged—this fatal professionalism. Millions of laymen have gone limp on evangelism—subtly or openly encouraged by the church's minister-centered tradition of many years. Think of how this limits the offering of Christ in a church with 300 members. The preacher or evangelist is only one person; he is limited to what one person can do. If every layman was offering Christ regularly, the evangelistic impact of that church would increase 300 times. Christ would be offered in places where the preacher never goes. He visits many homes and has many community contacts, but his congregation is composed of hundreds of laymen. They permeate and penetrate the life of the community and have countless opportunities to offer Christ.

Laymen have another big advantage over the pastor and professional evangelist—surprise. Everybody expects ministers and evangelists to talk about Christ. But when a layman offers Christ in the course of discussion over a business lunch or in a civic club committee meeting, people are astonished. Attention is transfixed by a layman's witness in a secular situation—giving that layman a golden opportunity closed to professional church workers.

Today the church is a sleeping giant. Millions of Methodists possess vast potential for offering Christ to a world which is perishing without Him. Holy Spirit move upon these mute millions! Transform each one into an offerer of Jesus Christ, so Your Church may accomplish the purpose for which You designed it.

QUESTIONS FOR DISCUSSION

1. *Have you ever "offered Christ" to anybody? What happened? Did you enjoy the experience? Was it difficult or easy?*

2. *What things must a person understand from the Gospel in order to present Christ properly?*

3. *What can happen if people "witness" only on the basis of their own experience, without awareness of Gospel principles about Christ, His mission, His promises, and His conditions?*

4. *Name some things that may prevent laymen from "offering Christ." Do ministers face any obstacles?*

5. *Explain the parable of the man who fished in his living room.*

6. *What causes a church to sit back and wait for people to come to church rather than going out with the Gospel to where unchurched people are living, working, and having fun?*

7. *Can you think of examples of your or your church's "going where the fish are"? What happened?*

8. *Does it seem coldhearted to offer Christ and then feel that one's responsibility is ended? In what way does this seem right? In what ways might it be wrong?*

9. *Can you do anything to convert another person? Who does the converting? What part of conversion is God's work and what part is man's?*

10. *Do you think that many people tend to think of evangelism as the business of pastors and evangelists rather than lay persons? What church practices encourage this way of thinking? Can you find any justification in the Bible for delegating the work of evangelism and witness to "professionals"?*

11. *Suppose you were the church caretaker who was confronted by a seeker late at night. How would you explain the way to become a Christian and to be saved?*

12. *Describe briefly the three main traits of John Wesley's evangelism, as described in this chapter.*

5

The Bible Is Your Favorite Book

THE SCENE: a seminary classroom.

"What is the basis for Christian missions?" the professor asks.

"The Great Commission given by Jesus as recorded in Matthew 28," replies a minister-to-be.

"But what if the so-called Great Commission is not really the words of Jesus?" the professor answers. "What if it is a propaganda statement added by the early church?"

The scene: a large sanctuary on Sunday morning.

The worship leader reads a section of Scripture from Luke. Then the preacher talks for twenty-five minutes, only briefly mentioning his Bible "text."

The scene: a pastor talking with his church school superintendent.

The pastor asks, "Why are you having the children memorize the Ten Commandments? Those are from the

Old Testament and we are Christians."

The scene: another seminary classroom.

A professor has been lecturing on "form criticism," a system of understanding the Bible by using techniques of literary analysis developed for understanding classical literature. During an hour's lecture there is no mention of the Holy Spirit. A student asks the professor, "Under form criticism, what part does the Holy Spirit have in the origination, transmission, and present interpretation of Scripture?"

After a pause, the professor answers: "None at all."

These four experiences happened to the author during the past ten years. Many similar incidents could be cited and countless variations could be given by thousands of Methodists. These incidents show that a major revolution has swept over Methodism in the past seventy-five years —a turning away from the Bible as authority for the church and for individual Christians. How far has this movement gone? Judge for yourself. Compare Methodism as you know it with the following statement by John Wesley, the original Methodist.

I have thought I am a creature of a day, passing through life as an arrow through the air. I am a spirit come from God, and returning to God: Just hovering over the great gulf; till, a few moments hence I am no more seen; I drop into an unchangeable eternity! I want to know one thing—the way to Heaven; how to land safe on that happy shore. God Himself has condescended to teach the way: For this very end He came from Heaven. He hath written it down in a book. Oh, give me that book! At any price give me the book of God! I have it: Here is knowledge enough for me. Let me be *homo unius libri* [man of one book]. Here then I am, far away from the busy ways of men. I sit down alone: Only God is here. In His presence I open, I read His book; for this end, to find the way to Heaven. Is

51

there a doubt concerning the meaning to the thing I read? Does anything appear dark or intricate? I lift up my heart to the Father of Lights: "Lord, is not Thy word, if any man lack wisdom, let him ask of God? Thou givest liberally, and upbraidest not. Thou hast said, if any be willing to do Thy will, he shall know. I am willing to do, let me know Thy will." I then search after and compare parallel passages of Scripture, comparing spiritual things with spiritual. I meditate thereon with all the attention and earnestness of which my mind is capable. If any doubt still remains, I consult those who are experienced in the things of God; and then the writings whereby, being dead, they yet speak. And what I thus learn, that I teach.

Abandonment of John Wesley's "high view" of Scripture is probably the most basic reason for Methodism's present weakness. Everywhere is vast ignorance of what the Bible really says; widespread false teaching; alarming silence about important Bible truths (when, for example, did you last hear a sermon about hell?). It is no coincidence that Methodists have most influenced the world when they, themselves, have been most influenced by the Bible. Power, courage to stand for truth, love of righteousness, wisdom, inner tranquility, perseverance and Christlikeness—all these are gifts which God gives to people who walk in the light of His eternal Word.

Because of all this, it is important to ask some basic questions about the Bible and to answer from the dynamic faith perspective of original Methodism.

Question One: *What is the Bible?*

First, it is the written record of God's relationship with people and nations from the time of Creation down to perhaps seventy years after the death and resurrection of Jesus Christ. God has preserved this historical record so that we might learn from it. So believers in every generation might profit from the victories, struggles, and failures of people long ago. Because it is an honest record, it contains bad as well as good things: King David's adultery, Jacob's trickery, Peter's triple denial of Jesus, the spiritual adultery of God's people in ancient Israel. God does not approve of these things because they are included in the Bible. They are reported through the tears of God because they happened, which makes the Bible as real as World War II and the assassination of John F. Kennedy.

Second, the Bible gives a broad outline of God's plan for the future of the universe. Many of the details are hidden by the Bible's mysterious symbolic language: "Then I looked, and I heard an eagle crying with a loud voice, as it flew in midheaven, 'Woe, woe, woe to those who dwell on the earth, at the blasts of the other trumpets which the three angels are about to blow!'" (Revelation 8: 13, RSV). Such symbolism cannot be understood with positive accuracy. But the Bible does make it unmistakably clear that someday God will conquer all evil. Someday He will establish His perfect Kingdom, in answer to our familiar prayer, "Thy kingdom come, Thy will be done on Earth as it is in Heaven."

The greatest Protestant interpreters of the Bible—John Calvin or Martin Luther—did not spend much time trying to penetrate the mysteries of the world's ending. But the broad outlines are evident in the Bible: The "blessed hope" of our Lord's coming again at the end of this age, the eventual liberation of the universe from sin's corrupting influence, and God's complete triumph over all forces and powers that now oppose Him.

This future dimension of faith is unknown to people who do not love and respect the Book of books. And to those who have fallen victim to skeptical critical philosophies which discredit the Bible's future warnings and promises.

Third, the Bible tells you plainly what you must do to be freed from sin, to belong to Jesus Christ, and to grow

53

as a Christian. This is known as the "way of salvation" and the path to perfection. In this respect, the Bible is a travel guide for our pilgrim's journey through this life and on into eternity.

Fourth, the Bible tells us what we need to know about Jesus Christ. The complete history of Jesus is revealed in the Bible: (1) how He existed with the Father and the Holy Spirit from before the beginning of the world, (2) how, at God's appointed time, Christ came to Earth as Jesus the God-man, (3) how living a fully human life He was tempted in every way that we are, but He did not sin, (4) how He showed us what it means to be perfectly human and at the same time perfect deity, (5) how He died upon the Cross to defeat evil and to pay for the sins of all who believe in Him, (6) how on the third day He was raised again by the Heavenly Father, (7) how He went back into Heaven where He now intercedes with God on behalf of every believer, (8) how He will return suddenly one day to pass final judgment upon the living and the dead, (9) how He will reign as King of kings and Lord of lords for ever and ever.

Fifth, the Bible is the Word which God has spoken to and through persons whom God chose to write down His eternal truth, to record His dealings with the world. For the benefit of future generations, God chose Isaiah, Jude, Peter, Paul, John, Amos, and many others. He allowed them to see great things. Then God sent His Spirit to breathe into their minds and consciousness His very truth. His message for the moment, in which was hidden implicitly the ultimate reality for all time to come.

While working this miracle known as "inspiration," God did not obliterate the humanness of the authors of Scripture. Instead, He creatively used their personalities and ways of thinking. These became God's vehicle for setting down His truth for the benefit of all generations. This inspiration of the Bible's authors makes their writing absolutely unique among all human writing. The writings which are included between Genesis 1 and Revelation 22 constitute God's full written revelation. As the Word on paper, Scripture complements and supplements the Word of God made flesh, Jesus Christ. They must be seen together as the fullness of God's total revelation—much as two sides of a coin represent the totality of that coin.

All human wisdom, written and spoken, is at best supplementary to Scripture, which towers above all other human expression. Scripture needs no completing; nor can anything be subtracted from Scripture without desecrating God's delicate balance of truth. This is why Jesus said, "Heaven and earth will pass away, but my words will not pass away" (Matthew 24: 35, RSV).

Precisely because the Bible *is* God's special revelation it has many mysteries. Nobody fully understands it all. Even those who study the Bible for a lifetime continue to find new and fresh truth emerging from its pages, truth about God, about the world, and about themselves. The Holy Spirit is the agent in this process of understanding the Bible. He inspired Scripture in the original. He has superintended the accurate transmission of God's truth down through the centuries, as the Bible was copied, recopied, translated, and paraphrased. And today when you read the Bible, the Holy Spirit will quicken your understanding and reveal new levels of God's truth, if you are a believer, or if you are seriously seeking after faith.

Question Two: *How can I believe the Bible if I can't understand it all?* A person reaches a point where he or she is able to say, "Lord, I believe it even though I don't understand everything. I do understand enough to recognize that You are speaking to me through this Book. It says so much about me that it cannot be the product of the human writer alone. It has the unmistakable depth of Your holy wisdom. Therefore I am prepared to say 'I believe!' although I do not yet understand it all. I shall trust You, Lord, to open the sacred page to my under-standing. By Your guidance I shall bring my life and thoughts into conformity with Your Word. And as this happens I shall be daily thankful to You for providing this blessed and unfailing guide."

Question Three: *What is the Bible's rightful place in my life and the life of the church today?*

The best answer comes from the Bible itself: "All Scripture is inspired by God and is [therefore] useful for teaching the truth, rebuking error, correcting faults, and giving instruction for right living, so that the man who serves God may be fully qualified and equipped to do every kind of good work" (II Timothy 3: 16, 17, TEV).

How does this work, practically? How does the authority of the Bible make itself felt?

Consider the matter of speaking in tongues. One group of Christians are tongues-speakers. In their enthusiasm, they insist that nobody is a Christian unless he or she can also speak in tongues; nobody has been "baptized" by the Holy Spirit unless that person speaks in tongues.

The church under Scriptural authority, asks these people, "Can you prove these claims by the plain teaching of Scripture?" No such proof can be furnished, so Bible Christians must reject all such exaggerated claims. This is "rebuking error" with Holy Scripture as supreme authority for right and wrong.

In the same church, other Christians deny that speaking in tongues can be a gift of God. They insist that all tongue-speaking be forbidden. Again the crucial question: "What say the Scriptures?" The answer is that tongue-speaking is listed as one of the authentic gifts of the Spirit (I Corinthians 12: 10). And the Scripture says, "Do not forbid speaking in tongues" (I Corinthians 14: 39b, RSV). So the antitongue-speaking critics, too, are out of bounds when their case is appealed to Scripture. The proper balance in this matter is clearly given in I Corinthians 14. Not all issues are so clearcut. Often Christians of the twentieth century face problems not specified in the Bible. What then?

The need is to draw from the plain teaching of Scripture, principles which can be applied, under the Holy Spirit's direction, to the problem. For example, air pollution. The Bible does not have a specific teaching on this matter. But Scripture does clearly teach that at Creation, God put man in charge of Earth—much as a company delegates supervision of a manufacturing plant to a general manager. One finds this Scriptural principle in Genesis 1: 26-30. The Holy Spirit helps the believer locate this principle and grasp its significance. Then the Spirit leads the Christian into action—which may well mean putting pressure on the city council to force a local factory to regulate its output of smoke.

Question Four: *Many people have different interpretations of what the Bible says. How can I interpret the Bible correctly?*

Professor Philip S. Watson, in his helpful book, *The Message of the Wesleys,* summarizes John Wesley's instructions on the matter:

"The general rule of interpreting Scripture is this: the literal sense of every text is to be taken, if it be not contrary to some other texts; but in that case the obscure text is to be interpreted by those which speak more plainly."

Let's apply this principle.

The birth of Jesus is described in Luke chapter 2. In Luke 1 we read how the angel Gabriel came to visit Mary. The angel announced, "Don't be afraid, Mary, because God has been gracious to you. You will become pregnant and give birth to a son, and you will name him Jesus" (Luke 1: 30, 31, TEV).

Mary, yet without a husband, asked in amazement, "I am a virgin. How, then, can this be?"

The angel answered: "The Holy Spirit will come on you, and God's power will rest upon you. For this reason the holy child will be called the Son of God."

Here, in the plainest way, is stated the truth that God is the biological Father of Jesus. This is known as the doctrine of "virgin birth." It is plainly taught in Scripture and so it is plainly true. To introduce theories which say anything else must be condemned as false teaching which directly contradicts the integrity of the Bible. When the Bible teaches something plainly, then it is true. That is the historic Methodist way.

But how about obscure texts? How are they to be understood? An analogy may be helpful. A man was camping. After dark he left his tent and went looking around the campsite to find his hat. His flashlight sent out a beam of light which pierced the darkness and revealed where the hat was.

When one Scripture is unclear then use another clear Scripture as the illuminating beam of light to penetrate the darkness. For example, Romans 7: 4, RSV, concludes ". . . in order that we may bear fruit for God." Suppose you wonder what is meant here by "fruit." To shed light on this matter, you turn to Galatians 5: 22, 23, RSV, which explains ". . . the fruit of the Spirit is love, joy, peace, patience, kindness, goodness, faithfulness, gentleness, self-control . . ."

To do this requires a growing, widening, deepening knowledge of the whole Bible. For both Old and New Testaments are understood in historic Methodist thinking as inspired Scripture. The Old Testament is God's revelation to people of the Old Testament period; the New Testament covers the period from the first coming of Christ until the Last Judgment. Both Testaments of the Bible are complementary and supplementary. Someone has said, "The New Testament is in the Old concealed and the Old by the New revealed."

A lady in my church once spoke of the angry God of the Old Testament and the loving God shown in the New Testament. I explained that God does not change character between the Testaments, but He has progressively revealed Himself more fully, climaxed in Jesus Christ. I asked for a chance to teach her Sunday school class the next week and I taught the love of God from the Old Testament and God's wrath from the New.

Understanding the proper relationship between the Testaments is one of the greatest needs. The Articles of Religion, one of the most important definitions of Methodist doctrine developed by John Wesley from the Articles of the Church of England, says this about the Old-New Testamental relationship:

ARTICLE VI—Of the Old Testament.

The Old Testament is not contrary to the New; for both in the Old and New Testament everlasting life is offered to mankind by Christ, who is the only Mediator between God and men, being both God and man. Wherefore they are not to be heard who feign that the old fathers did look only for transitory promises. Although the Law given from God by Moses as touching ceremonies and rites doth not bind Christians, nor ought the civil precepts thereof of necessity be received in any Commonwealth; yet notwithstanding, no Christian whatsoever is free from the obedients of the commandments which are called moral.

Professor Watson gives this summary of John Wesley's practical instruction for Methodists learning the Bible:

"If you desire to read the Scriptures in such a manner as may most effectually answer this end, would it not be advisable (1) to set apart a little time, if you can, every morning and evening for the purpose? (2) At each time, if you have leisure, to read a chapter out of the Old, and one out of the New Testament; if you cannot do this, to take a single chapter or part of one? (3) to read this with a single eye to know the whole will of God, and a fixed resolution to do it? In order to know His will, you should (4) have a constant eye to the analogy of faith, the connexion and harmony there is between those grand, fundamental doctrines, original sin, justification by faith, the new birth, inward and outward holiness. (5) Serious and earnest prayer should be constantly used before we consult the oracles of God, seeing "Scripture can only be understood by the same Spirit whereby it was given." Our reading should likewise be closed with prayer, that what we read may be written in our hearts. (6) It might also be of use, if while we read we were frequently to pause and examine ourselves by what we read, both with regard to our hearts and lives."

A closing caution: Today there are many false teachings about the Bible. Here are some of the most common errors that may be heard in sermons or read in printed material:

1. The Bible is not historically true; it reports things which may not really have happened. This tears the Scripture out of history and makes it a fairy tale.

2. The Bible contains many additions by the early church. To get the "authentic" teachings of "original" Scripture the Bible must be "demythologized." This means that the interpreter is free to reject anything not compatible to his ideas of science or contemporary philosophy. This allows each person to create his or her own Bible.

3. Jesus is the full revelation of God, separate from the Scriptures. This is like dividing the front from the back side of a coin. God's Word-in-flesh (Jesus) is inseparable from God's Word-in-words (Scripture), for they point to Him and He fulfills them.

4. The Old Testament is sub-Christian and therefore should be ignored. This is one of the oldest heresies and has been widely promoted by so-called "liberal" scholarship, much of which is, in reality, neither liberal nor scholarship.

5. The Bible is not "relevant" today. Therefore one ignores it and learns what God is doing through the television and the onrush of daily events. Someone who claims the Bible is "not relevant" does not know what is in the Bible. The daily news is transient and lacking in enduring truth connected to the ultimate realities of existence. To trade tv for the Bible is a poor exchange.

6. Everybody has a different idea of what the Bible says, so everybody is free to interpret the Bible however he or she pleases.

On many things, people do differ in understanding the Bible. But if the Bible is taken to mean what it plainly says, then it contains a great many absolute truths which can be agreed upon—that God is personal, that Christ is God-in-the-flesh, that He died for sinners, that He rose bodily from the grave, that human nature is deeply perverted from God's original plan, that God has full control over the laws of nature—these are only a few of the obvious truths on which Bible Christians can and do agree. All we need to know to be saved and to grow as Christians is plainly stated in the Scriptures.

7. The church created the Scriptures. Not so—God created the Scriptures. The truths revealed therein are His. Being the truths of Christ, Scriptures are actually the source of the church. It is not the right of the church to distort or ignore the Scriptures but to conform to them gladly, understand them, interpret them to the world gladly and completely.

The place of the Bible in Methodist faith and life is clearly described in the Articles of Religion which John Wesley sent to guide Methodists in America. These so-called "historic landmarks" contain Article V, as follows:

"The Holy Scriptures contain all things necessary to salvation; so that whatsoever is not read therein, nor may be proved thereby, is not to be required of any man that it should be believed as an article of faith, or be thought requisite or necessary to salvation. In the name of the Holy Scriptures we do understand those canonical* books of the Old and New Testament of whose authority was never any doubt in the Church. [Here follows a list of Old Testament books, not counting the apocrypha.] All the books of the New Testament, as they are commonly received, we do receive and account canonical.

*Canonical: Declared as the inspired writings by various church councils which, under the leading of the Holy Spirit, confirmed the seal of divine authenticity upon certain works which had, by their superior power, insight and wisdom, proved themselves to be supernaturally inspired.

QUESTIONS FOR DISCUSSION

1. *What is meant by "the Bible is authority"?*

2. *Do you agree or disagree with the statement:* "Each person gives the Bible authority, or not, in his own life"?

3. *How many of the common mistakes about the Bible can you remember from those which were briefly explained in this chapter? Have you ever encountered these mistakes? Have any of them crept into your mind?*

4. *What did John Wesley mean when he said that a Methodist is nothing more or less than a Bible Christian? Is there any other kind of Christian?*

5. *What are the three ways that the Holy Spirit is involved in the Bible and its study?*

6. *Why does reading the Bible make some people feel guilty and others happy?*

7. *Can you describe the difference in attitude toward the Bible between* (1) *mature believers,* (2) *nominal church members,* (3) *unbelievers?*

8. *How would you answer if somebody said, "The only Bible that is correct is the King James Version"?*

9. *Can you remember when you received from the Bible either warning, comfort, or a correction on your thought or conduct?*

10. *It has been said often that a person cannot continue as a Christian without regular and serious study of the Bible. Do you agree?*

11. *What is the proper relationship between the Old and New Testaments?*

12. *Suppose you are not able to understand everything you read in the Bible. Does this mean you cannot say "I believe the Bible is true"? Explain.*

6

You Are Going on to Perfection

IT IS METHODIST ordination time.

A group of ministers-to-be stand self-consciously in front of the annual conference delegates. The bishop asks a series of old questions, established by John Wesley. Three of these sound strange to modern ears:

"Are you going on to perfection?"

"Do you expect to be made perfect . . . in this life?"

"Are you earnestly striving after it (perfection)?"

These questions bring some smiles in the audience— and some deep wondering. Going on to perfection? Becoming perfect now? In this life?

The doctrine of Christian perfection has always raised a lot of questions. This is natural because it is one of the great mysteries of our faith. But from the beginning Methodists have emphasized Christian perfection. Visiting the early Methodist societies, Wesley often observed that lack of spiritual progress was due to lack of emphasis on

Christian perfection, also known as "entire sanctification." This doctrine historically distinguished Methodists among other Christians as double-predestination historically distinguished the Presbyterians.

"It is our deep-seated conviction that God's grace is sufficient to make us perfect in love," wrote United Methodist Bishop Mack Stokes in *Major Methodist Beliefs*. "Just as our commitment can be sure, our sincerity in love can be perfect. All Methodists agree, then, that the grace of God is fully able to work within our hearts to make them pure and loving and wise (see I Thess. 5: 23). It is our earnest prayer that we may be made perfect in love day by day. And if Methodism loses this passion for Christian perfection, it will not only betray its heritage, it will neglect its mission in the world today."

Jesus himself sets the very highest standard of perfection for His followers: "Be ye therefore perfect, even as your Father which is in heaven is perfect" (Matthew 5: 48). The Greek word used here for "perfect" means completed works; finished product, lacking nothing; full maturity.

In one of his last books, *The Unshakeable Kingdom and the Unchanging Person,* (Nashville: Abingdon Press, 1972, pp. 153-4) the late E. Stanley Jones, world famous Methodist missionary-evangelist, wrote these words of comment upon Matthew 5: 48:

"Be ye perfect." What did He (Jesus) mean by it? Therefore is the key word. It points back. He was talking about loving your enemies. The word points back to this kind of perfection, perfection in love. It is possible to be perfect in love without being perfect in character or service. The word "as" could be translated "since"—since your Heavenly Father is perfect as God, you can be perfect as a child of God. Tagore, the Indian poet, said: "Everything in nature lifts up strong hands unto perfection." So in the Christian faith the perfection is patterned after the most beautiful and the strongest character who ever lived—Jesus Christ. So the perfection offered saves us from perfectionism by making it a by-product of loyalty to Jesus Christ, so that it is not a self-conscious striving after perfection, but a perfection after the pattern of the most balanced character who ever lived, infinite sanity blended with infinite sanctity and motivated by love—infinite love. Perfectionism is self-centered, therefore self-defeating. Perfection in love is others-regarding, therefore self-dedicating, therefore self-fulfilling and self-releasing."

The power to reach perfection is Jesus Christ. The apostle Paul said, "I can do all things through Christ which strengtheneth me" (Philippians 4: 13). And, "Yet not I, but Christ liveth in me: and the life which I now live in the flesh I live by the faith of the Son of God, who loved me, and gave himself for me" (Galatians 2: 20).

The term "perfection" means "pure love reigning alone in the heart and life. This is the whole of Scriptural perfection," wrote Wesley in *A Plain Account of Christian Perfection*. This is not just human love at its best but, instead, is God's love conveyed by the Holy Spirit (Romans 5: 5). And again: "Christian perfection is that love of God and our neighbor which delivers from all sin. This is received merely by faith. It is given instantaneously, in one moment. We are to expect it not at death, but every moment. Now is the accepted time, now is the day of salvation."

Our Lord gave this capsule definition: "Thou shalt love the Lord thy God with all thy heart, and with all thy soul, and with all thy mind . . . Thou shalt love thy neighbour as thyself" (Matthew 22: 37, 39).

Such perfect love, through Jesus, should be the constant hope and expectation of every Methodist. To be perfection-bound is God's normal way of Christian development. Wrote Methodist Bishop Francis J. McConnell: "It is the manifest duty of the Christian to aim at being perfect, just as it is the duty of the scientist to strive after perfect knowledge, or the duty of an artist to seek the perfect expression of beauty."

God is the Sanctifier. He can work the miracle of perfecting you in an instant. "With men this is impossible; but with God all things are possible" (Matthew 19: 26). Because John Wesley believed this literally, he urged Methodists to expect the perfection miracle at any moment.

One man, now a leading Christian educator, was converted as a teenager. Four days later God worked in his heart a miracle of perfect love. It was a precious and holy moment, and it set the tone for a lifetime of usefulness to God.

Wesley said that although such miracles can and sometimes do happen, the usual sanctification experience comes sometime after conversion. The Methodist, therefore, remains ready to receive God's gifts and miracles whenever and however God chooses to bestow them, instantly or gradually.

It's a mystery beyond the mind's grasp how Christian perfection can be both an instant work and a process—a long journey. But this is the historic Methodist witness.

The apostle Paul helps us at this point. Writing to the Philippians he declared, "Not that I have already obtained this [Christ's resurrection] or am already perfect; but I press on to make it [perfection] my own, because Christ Jesus has made me his own . . . but one thing I do, forgetting what lies behind and straining forward to what lies ahead, I press on toward the goal for the prize of the upward call of God in Christ Jesus. Let those of us who are mature [same Greek word as "perfect" above] be thus minded; and if in anything you are otherwise minded, God will reveal that also to you. Only let us hold true to what we have attained" (Philippians 3: 12-16, RSV).

This passage contains both the "not yet" and the "already happened" views of perfection. Clearly, Paul is not satisfied that he is already fully perfect. He is moving steadily toward God's high goal. But a level of sanctification has been reached. He uses the same Greek word, *teleos,* to describe his present state of Christian maturity as was used at the start of this passage to indicate a state of perfect-ness which is still beyond him.

All Christians walk the razor's edge when it comes to perfection. On one side is a precipice of discouragement. Many fall into it by comparing themselves with Christ— and feeling despair. On the other side of perfection is a deep gorge known as complacency. Some slip into this after feeling they can never attain the perfection of Christ. They settle back "just as I am" with never a thought of victory over habitual sin and weakness. Others fall into this gorge because they have too superficial a view of what God's perfection involves. They conform to external rules like tithing, going to church, not smoking, not swearing or drinking, etc. Keeping these regulations, they feel Christian perfection has been achieved—when in reality the deep inner recesses of prejudice, emotion, and selfishness remain untouched.

E. Stanley Jones said that justification (i.e., first salvation) happens when you give Christ control over your outward life, and that sanctification (i.e., full and completed salvation) is Christ's Lordship extended over the subconscious—where lurk hidden motives, monstrous feelings, and thoughts sometimes ugly and wicked.

Here is where the process idea of perfection comes in. The Christian life is seen as a whole series of surrenders, by which subterranean caverns of self are opened to Christ's cleansing presence. The indwelling Holy Spirit makes a believer conscious of something yet closed to Jesus. A long period of conviction and struggle may follow this realization—climaxed by a new and fuller surrender of this particular area. Thus perfection may develop through a continuing series of works of God's grace subsequent to salvation.

A woman, age 45, had been converted at 16. She loved Christ and had a deep and mature faith. Love was very evident in her family, friends, and neighbors. But she had never been able to let other people, even those close to her, know how she felt about many things. This Christian woman lived corked-up emotionally. Inner tension kept her from being the person God wanted her to be.

A lay witness mission came to her church. In one of the discussion groups she learned that other people had this same problem. The Holy Spirit was active that night, and He touched her during the meeting. Her inhibitions melted away, and she found herself able, for the first time, to speak honestly about her feelings. That night she and her husband talked for hours. It was the frankest conversation they'd had in twenty married years.

What had happened?

The woman had opened to Jesus' cleansing power a part of her life never before yielded. Because Jesus became Lord of her feelings, she can now be honest. Sometimes people misunderstand her. Sometimes her honesty is painful. But God knows that her intention is pure. Her motive has been cleansed by Christ, and that matters to God.

"Christian perfection, for Wesley, means only one thing, and that is purity of motive," writes United Methodist Bishop William R. Cannon in *The Theology of John Wesley*.

> The love of God, freed entirely from all the corruptions of natural desire and emancipated completely from any interest in self or in any other person or thing apart from God, guides unhindered every thought and every action of a man's life. In body and mind the perfect Christian is still finite; he makes mistakes in judgment as long as he lives; these mistakes in judgment occasion mistakes in practice, and mistakes in practice often have bad moral consequences. Thus perfection in the sense of infallibility does not exist on the face of the Earth.

In grasping the importance of Christian perfection, sin's meaning must be considered. The Methodist understanding, given by Wesley and passed down through Methodist generations, is that sin is known breaking of the known will of God. For example, knowing it is wrong to cheat on your expense account, but doing it anyway. Or knowing that your gossip may hurt somebody, but gossiping anyway. Or failing to praise and thank God when you know that praise and thanks are His due.

Some people think this is too narrow a view of sin. They argue that sin is any breaking of God's laws, whether you know it or not. A speeder, they say, is arrested even if he does not know that he is driving 45 in a 35 m.p.h. zone.

Methodist realism declares that known sin is a big enough problem. Limiting sin to the things we know we have done wrong (or failed to do) leaves plentiful grounds for conviction and repentance. And it seems logical that God will hold us more responsible for the sins we know about.

As you turn to Jesus, you turn away from sin. He lifts the believer to Himself, where sin cannot exist any more than bacteria can live in boiling water. Sin is swallowed up in Jesus' mighty power, like a bottle of ink would disappear in the ocean.

Astronauts going to the moon discovered Earth's gravitational pull getting weaker as they traveled farther and farther into space. Finally the gravitational pull of the moon became stronger and Earth's attractive force faded out.

Movement toward Christ is "going on to perfection." His gravitational pull becomes stronger than the sinward tugging of the old nature. When the holiness of God becomes the dominant force within you, you experience Christian perfection.

It means God's love and power lifting you above the

"self" of which you are ashamed.

It means nailing to Christ's Cross all that is un-God-like about you. Putting it to death with Christ.

It means, afterward, living under the control of the mind of Christ.

Fantastic! Incredible! But it can happen—indeed it will happen if you sincerely ask God for the gift of perfect love. That is why Methodists pray for one another: "May the God of peace himself sanctify you wholly; and may your spirit and soul and body be kept sound and blameless at the coming of our Lord Jesus Christ. He who calls you [to perfection] is faithful, and he will do it" (I Thessalonians 5: 23, 24, RSV).

> Jesus, Thine all-victorious love
>   Shed in my heart abroad.
> Then shall my soul no longer rove
>   Rooted and fixed in God.
>
> Refining fire, go through my heart
>   Illuminate my soul.
> Scatter Thy life through every part
>   And sanctify the whole.—*Charles Wesley*

QUESTIONS FOR DISCUSSION

1. *Did you ever meet a Christian who seemed to be perfect?*

2. *Why do you think many Methodists fail to emphasize Christian perfection?*

3. *Would most Methodist people today be glad to hear preachers urging them to be "going on to perfection"? What reasons can you give to support your opinion?*

4. *What is the historic Methodist understanding of "sin"? Does the Bible support this?*

5. *Critics have said that the Methodist idea of sin makes it easy for people to rationalize that "I made a mistake, but I did not sin." What do you say about this?*

6. *Can a person be perfectly motivated by Jesus' love, and still make errors and mistakes? Do you think God considers a person's true motives more important than success in carrying out the intention perfectly? Can you*

defend your opinion from the Bible?

7. Have you ever seen evidence of God's power enabling a believer to overcome an old sin? Will God keep you from sinning in the future?

8. Something happens at the time of conversion that lays the foundation for "growth in grace" and the experience of entire sanctification. What is it?

9. Why did Jesus command believers to be as perfect as God is perfect (Matthew 5: 48)? Is this goal attainable? How? Does God make demands that He does not expect His children to fulfill?

10. Think honestly about your own life and especially your present state as a Christian. Are you "going on to perfection"? Have you stopped growing toward the likeness of Jesus Christ?

11. What signs would indicate that a person has "perfect love"?

12. In the clearest way you can, explain what "Christian perfection" is.

7

You Seek Blessed Assurance

WE LIKE TO SING the familiar hymn by Fanny Crosby, the blind Methodist:

Blessed assurance, Jesus is mine
  Oh what a foretaste of glory divine!
Heir of salvation, purchase of God
  Born of His Spirit, washed in His Blood.

Perfect submission, all is at rest.
  I in my Savior am happy and blest
Watching and waiting, looking above
  Filled with His goodness, lost in His love.

Full assurance became real to me one early morning in East Texas. I was in the middle of a week-long revival. That morning there had been a Bible study group to teach. During the afternoon we had visited people in the little town. That evening there was preaching and talking with people afterward. Finally, I had visited until midnight with the revival songleader, a vital young man who was staying with me in the home of a church family.

I went to bed tired, but thanking God for the day. Suddenly I was awakened from my sleep. My watch said it was 1:30 AM. Outside, a mockingbird was warbling, but all else was quiet. The moonlight was beaming in my open window and I knew with "the eye of the heart" it was time to pray. I knelt down by the bed and a great wave of thankfulness to God swept over me. It was something like I had experienced six years before when I became a Christian—only this time it was far deeper, more intense, and more specific.

God assured me, "I will never leave you. I will be with you always." Again and again this was impressed on my mind and soul. It is hard to describe this inner awareness of love and trust in which I was immersed. Certain Bible truths were seared indelibly into my soul. I heard no voice, but God spoke to my innermost being: "You are mine. My child. For ever and ever. Now the riches of Christ are all yours. There's a place in Heaven reserved especially for you. No matter what obstacles you face from now on, I will bring you safely through. Together, we shall overcome."

It was a deep assurance of God's love for me. Of His acceptance of me through Christ. Of His great kindness and mercy, which I did not deserve. It was my personal experience of Romans 8: 15b-17 (RSV):

When we cry "Abba! Father!" it is the Spirit himself bearing witness with our spirit that we are children of God, and if children, then heirs, heirs of God and fellow heirs with Christ, provided we suffer with him in order that we may also be glorified with him.

Other Methodists have told me about times when God expressed to them a wonderfully deeper assurance of His personal love and concern. Indeed, real Methodism has always empasized that each believer should expect to know that he or she has been saved; that all sin has been

73

cleansed by the blood of Christ; that through Jesus, he or she shall not perish but shall live everlastingly; that he or she is now God's child through Jesus Christ.

"Blessed Assurance," therefore, is one of the most proper Methodist hymns. The idea of assurance is common among the hymns written by Charles Wesley. Here are just two examples:

My God, I am Thine
    What a comfort divine
What a blessing to know that Jesus is mine!
    In the Heavenly Lamb
Thrice happy I am
    And my heart it doth dance at the sound of His
        name.
Also:
Wherefore in never-ceasing prayer
    My soul to Thy continual care
I faithfully commend
    Assured that Thou through life shalt save
And show Thyself beyond the grave
    My everlasting Friend.

But the experience of "Blessed Assurance" is no longer common among many church people today. Ask yourself: "Do you know that Christ died for you? That you are saved? That you are a 'child of the King'?" Is your answer "I don't know" or "I'm not sure"?

We live in an age of uncertainty about spiritual things. Vagueness and nonassurance seem normal in churches today. A person who declares confidently, "I know in whom I have believed" may be considered eccentric.

This modern nonassurance is foreign to the Bible—and to genuine Methodism. Firm, Christ-rooted assurance is a basic Bible doctrine. Here are just a few examples:

"Be still, and know that I am God" (Psalm 46: 10).

"Indeed I count everything as loss because of the surpassing worth of knowing Christ Jesus my Lord . . . that I may know him and the power of his resurrection" (Philippians 3: 8, 10, RSV).

"I am not ashamed, for I know whom I have believed and I am sure that he is able to guard until that Day what has been entrusted to me" (II Timothy 1: 12, RSV).

". . . that you may know that I am the Lord in the midst of the earth" (Exodus 8: 22, RSV).

"For I know that my Redeemer lives, and at last he will stand upon the earth; and after my skin has been thus destroyed, then without my flesh I shall see God" (Job 19: 25, 26, RSV).

The Bible leaves not the slightest sense of doubt that firm assurance is a part of proper faith. In fact, without growing, deepening assurance is not Bible faith. Methodists starting with John Wesley have strongly doubted that a person could be a Christian without some definite sense of assurance.

How does proper assurance come to believers?

Conversion cannot take place without a triple assurance: (1) that I need Jesus Christ, (2) He is able to forgive my sins and get my life back onto the right track— God's track. These beginning certainties are necessary before a person turns to Christ. This first or preliminary assurance centers on awareness of the seeker's own needs and inadequacies. Simultaneously the Holy Spirit brings confidence that "Christ is the answer." This double certainty brings the seeker to the point where a third aspect of assurance is born: (3) that the blood of Jesus Christ has in fact made me clean from every past sin. With a beginner's spiritual understanding you know that you are accepted as a child of God, "just as I am without one plea, but that Thy blood was shed for me."

The Holy Spirit first produced conviction necessary to bring you to the point of conversion. (This is known to Methodists as prevenient grace—the love and mercy of God reaching out to draw lost sinners to saving trust in Christ.) After this happens, the Spirit begins working with the new believer as a Christian. Now the Spirit leads the convert toward the experience of perfect love and full assurance.

As you make your Christian journey, more and more certainty develops. The Holy Spirit upsets some of your old certainties, but He gives you new assurances in exchange. Better ones!

Before I became a Christian, I had absolute assurance in myself. I had no assurance that God was real, that He was personally involved in the world, or that He cared about me.

Becoming a Christian marked the first real break in my self-assurance and the dawning of the divine assurance that "Jesus loves even me." After conversion the Holy Spirit gradually reversed my center of assurance. He revealed to me the depth of my sin and I began to see that in myself I had no ground for assurance. I began to see Christ as the only reliable ground for my trust. Thus God destroyed false assurance and gave me a new and better confidence. Assurance grew that He is wonderful. That His grace (kindness and favor I did not deserve) is truly amazing. My blessed assurance grew stronger while my unblessed assurance grew weaker. What a miracle! How much better to trust in One who doesn't change. Who is able to accomplish all things according to His will. Who saves to the uttermost. Who wants to be my Father in Heaven.

I prayed—and the answers came. Surprisingly. Ingeniously. Adequately. This happened over and over—and so assurance developed that "my God will supply every need . . . according to his riches in glory in Christ Jesus (Philippians 4: 19, RSV).

Being a pastor forces one to trust God. The Methodist and United Methodist pastoral ministry drew me steadily toward full assurance of God's wondrous love and power.

Through many experiences God deepened my trust in His adequacy for everything.

A favorite Bible promise, proved over and over, is:

If any of you [believers] lacks wisdom, let him ask God who gives to all men generously and without reproaching, and it will be given him. But let him ask in faith, with no doubting, for he who doubts is like a wave of the sea that is driven and tossed by the wind. For that person must not suppose that a double-minded man, unstable in all his ways, will receive anything from the Lord" (James 1: 5-8, RSV).

I had just been ordained a Methodist deacon in the Rock River Annual Conference of The Methodist Church. As a supply preacher, with one year of seminary completed, I was filling the pulpit of a small country church. One Saturday the phone rang. It was the church lay leader: "Please come quickly. There's been a terrible tragedy. Two of our members have been found murdered. They think the teenage son is guilty."

Soon I was walking through the home of the murdered couple. The gruesome, blood-spattered basement was a slaughterhouse. The couple's bodies had been found in the trunk of the family car three miles away. Their teenage son was at the county jail being questioned.

The phone rang. It was the sheriff: "The boy just confessed. He wants to see the minister."

As I drove to the county seat I wondered: What can I say to a teenager who has just killed both his parents? Suddenly I knew that I had nothing to say. The familiar words from James flashed into my mind. I prayed, "Lord, I don't have to tell You that I am lacking in wisdom right now. In just a few minutes, I'll be walking into that jail cell. Please give me the right words to say—Your words, Your wisdom. Lord, I'm counting on You . . . and I thank You for hearing this prayer. In Jesus' name."

The cell door opened and there sat the seventeen-year-old boy, huddled in the corner, sobbing. He looked so small. He grabbed my hand and moaned, "Oh God. God. God."

Suddenly, I was speaking—and yet not I. Through my lips God spoke to this young killer. Telling him that even the murder of his parents was not beyond God's ability to forgive. That the blood of Christ would cleanse him that very moment. That God's mercy in Christ was available—even to murderers of parents. That God loved him right now.

Into my insufficiency, God moved with marvelous all-sufficiency. Over and over God has done this for me, producing a deep assurance that my Heavenly Father's love is real—and very practical.

When our five children were small, we had a plastic swimming pool in our back yard. We would turn on the garden hose and in about one hour the pool would be full of water.

This can be a parable of assurance. As a new Christian you begin to know a kindergarten assurance about God. The hose is turned on, so to speak, when you first come to Jesus and begin to know Him. Thus the filling of assurance begins. As you live close to Jesus, you have more and more experiences that prove His promises are true. This increases your assurance until eventually, like the pool filled with water, you become filled with assurance. Then, as overflow, God gives you the experience of full assurance described in Romans 8: 16.

First or beginning assurance usually comes the moment you become a Christian. Sometime later, full or mature assurance is given by the Holy Spirit. A fair period of time usually separates mature assurance from what you experienced when you were saved—or justified by faith.

Have you experienced this "blessed assurance"? If so, it is a cause for daily thanksgiving. If you have to answer "No" or "I'm not sure," then you have reason to question whether you ever really surrendered your life to Jesus Christ. Methodists have traditionally believed that an absence of assurance may well mean an absence of salvation. God alone is the judge. But if your assurance is dim or nonexistent, you would be wise to ask God about this in prayer.

Perhaps you have beginner's assurance, and the taste has whetted your appetite for more. God delights to give good gifts to His children (Matthew 7: 11), so now would be a good time to ask God to crown your Christian life with a glorious confirmation that "I'm a child of the King!"

If full assurance is yours, take this opportunity to praise and thank God for all that He is, and all that He means to you.

QUESTIONS FOR DISCUSSION

1. *If you had to measure your own assurance on a scale from 0 (none) to 10 (full), where would you stand?*

2. *What difference has assurance made: in your home? your daily work? your church?*

3. *Describe the difference between "full assurance" and the assurance people have when they first became Christians.*

4. *Is assurance a feeling? Can you have assurance without feelings?*

5. *How does a person's assurance grow stronger and deeper? Has this happened in your life?*

6. *What is the relationship between assurance and depending upon God? Suppose a person never depended upon God. Could that person have assurance? Explain.*

7. *What would you say if someone said, "If you don't feel assurance, then you are not a Christian"? What does the Bible say to prove or disprove this idea?*

8. *What are some specific assurances that God gives to believers?*

9. *The author described a change in the kind of assurance he knew before and after he became a Christian. Can you describe this shift in the focus of assurance?*

10. *Is it possible to have false assurance? If so, what might this be? Can you give examples?*

11. *Why is lack of certainty (nonassurance) so common today—even among church people?*

12. *Can you remember some Bible verses which show certainty of faith? Others which show doubt, hesitance to believe, uncertainty, nonassurance?*

8

Your Top Priority Is God

LIFE IS A MATTER of priorities. What you put first, second, third, fourth, and fifth show what you consider most important. Your real values are clearly revealed by the persons or causes which take your time, your energy, and your money.

A woman celebrity once told a writer that she owned 103 pairs of shoes. "Looking good" was her top priority. How she impressed people was this famous woman's number one concern.

A minister is most concerned about keeping on good terms with the church hierarchy. His theology and his personal convictions are quickly silenced if they cause any disagreement with those who are responsible for his appointment to important committees, and moving him to bigger churches with nicer parsonages. This minister's first priority is not God, but advancement of his career.

A woman devotes her life to chasing dirt. Always the

piano in her living room must be dust-free. Always she struggles to keep finger marks off the door, children off the good sofa, and her sons' bedrooms as neat and orderly as hospital operating rooms. She has a compulsion for cleanliness and order. Cleanliness is not next to godliness; it is her god because it is her first priority. (That, incidentally, is a practical definition of your god: whatever is most important to you.)

God cares about your priorities because they reveal what you believe to be important. Jesus was talking about this when He told His disciples to "seek first his [God's] kingdom and his righteousness" (Matthew 6: 33, RSV). In other words, God must be first priority for followers of Jesus Christ.

The whole Bible says this. "You shall have no other gods before me" (Exodus 20: 3, RSV) is the very first Commandment. Jesus expressed it this way: "You shall love the Lord your God with all your heart, and with all your soul, and with all your mind" (Matthew 22: 37, RSV).

All. First priority.

It is not an oversimplification to say that the Bible's message is (1) God demands to be first, (2) people and nations often fail to put God first, (3) this always results in disaster—personal and national, and (4) God's plan to save us from wrong priorities centers around His only begotten Son. Christ came to Earth, died on the Cross and rose from the grave in order to enable those who obey Him to put God first in all things.

—Such as our attitudes toward neighbors.

—Such as our desire for fairness in business dealings.

—Such as our standards of right and wrong for our children.

—Such as our emotions.

—Such as how we use our spare time.

In all these things Satan wants you to put something

else ahead of God. Any substitute will do: love for your children, pride in your house, desire for cultural refinement, loyalty to class, race, or country. You please Satan whenever you allow anything to become more important than God—measured by how you allocate your time, your energies, your enthusiasm, and your money. God can be pleased in only one way—putting Him first.

There is within each of us a tug-of-war over priorities, the real battlefield of the Christian life. Satan tugs at you to put yourself first; God tugs at you to put first His Kingdom and His righteousness. The Christian is not absolutely released from this tension until death lifts him or her into Heaven where Satan has no influence . . . where all is love, praise and worship of God.

Until a person belongs to God through Jesus Christ, Satan sets the priorities. Being converted or born again means turning from Satan to God. It is something like what happened in World War II, when the Allied armies invaded Europe. They landed on the Normandy Coast and in a few days won a permanent beachhead. When this happened Hitler lost the war—even though many battles still had to be fought before the Nazis formally surrendered.

Our spiritual war is won when Christ establishes a firm beachhead: when we confess Him as Savior and ask Him to enter in as Lord. But many hard spiritual battles remain to be fought before "sin's fierce war shall cease." This combat is known as the Christian life. The battlefield is the Christian's daily priorities. The crucial question: Will God come first, second, or third?

Once Jesus visited the home of Martha and Mary. Martha bustled around in the kitchen getting a fancy dinner while Mary "sat at the Lord's feet and listened to his teaching" (Luke 10: 39, RSV). Later Jesus explained, "Mary has chosen the good portion." He commended her for having made a wiser choice in priorities than

Martha, who put cooking a meal ahead of listening to Jesus.

This story of wrong and right priorities is relived every Sunday morning when the sermon runs ten minutes long and some churchgoers become angry because this interferes with plans for their big Sunday dinner.

The superreligious Pharisees criticized Jesus because He and His disciples ate with ordinary people, "tax collectors and sinners." The religious leaders were criticizing Jesus' social priority: giving time to riffraff instead of associating only with "good people." Jesus corrected the Pharisees' wrong priority in human relations: "Tax collectors [thieves] and the harlots go into the kingdom of God before you" (Matthew 21: 31, RSV). Also, "Those who are well have no need of a physician, but those who are sick. Go and learn what this means, 'I [God] desire mercy, and not sacrifice.' For I [Jesus] came not to call the righteous, but sinners" (Matthew 9: 12, 13, RSV).

Once the disciples asked Jesus if He wasn't hungry after spending a long day without eating. They were giving top priority to meeting the needs of the body. Jesus replied, "My food is to do the will of him who sent me" (John 4: 34, RSV). Satisfying body needs deserved a lower priority than the tasks which God has set. As Jesus had said earlier: "Man shall not live by bread alone" (Luke 4: 4, RSV).

Jesus established a whole new order of priorities for His followers and for His Church. As followers of Jesus, Methodists at their best are determined to reorganize their life priorities; to put God's will, truth, and righteousness ahead of everything else.

John Wesley expressed this idea in his classic *Character of a Methodist*: ". . . God is the joy of the Methodist's heart, the desire of his soul, which cries out constantly, 'Whom have I in Heaven but You, Lord? There is nothing on Earth that I desire but You, my God and my all. You

are the strength of my life. You, Lord, are all that I need
. . .' "

Attempting seriously to carry out Jesus' reversal of priorities has made real Methodists stand out from nominal Christians, and from the unbelieving world. To put God first—even to desire this—automatically makes any group a "peculiar people." For most people ignore God completely or relegate Him to an insignificant corner of their lives.

To accomplish this radical reversal of life priorities, Christians need guidance and discipline. Jesus showed this in His disciplined life of prayer, worship, and service, which should set the pattern for His disciples. Without these disciplines there is little chance of getting to the place where you can say with Jesus, "nevertheless not my will, but thine, be done" (Luke 22: 42, RSV). The so-called spiritual disciplines of prayer, worship, Bible study, sacraments, and Christian friendship are required to keep God Number One in Methodists' hearts.

In John Wesley's time, Methodists took the sacrament of Holy Communion in the Church of England on Sunday morning. Then, on Sunday afternoon, they gathered for special preaching services in homes, public buildings, and in plain chapels built and maintained by the Methodists. As the week progressed, every Methodist came to a "class meeting" with perhaps ten or twelve others and an appointed leader. They sang hymns. They prayed. They studied the Bible. They took an offering (again). They examined themselves and one another to see what progress, or failures, as Christians they had experienced during the week.

Other meetings were often required. No wonder Methodists were considered odd. God came first in their priorities, and this was enough to label anyone a fanatic—then and now.

Because they wanted God to be first, Methodists laid

down strict rules for themselves. Those who did not accept these disciplines could not become or remain Methodists. Unwillingness to be a disciplined Christian was considered a sign that something other than God had become the "backslider's" first priority. Methodism at its best has not tolerated religious pretenders, because the very idea of inactive or lukewarm Christians is a contradiction—like cold fire or dark sunlight.

The *General Rules of Methodism* must be seen in this light—not as articles of faith, but as practical guides for helping serious Christians win the battle to keep God first. These rules recognize that people are weak and need guidance to overcome the everpresent power of evil.

No one can understand what it means to be a Methodist without pondering the historic General Rules. For this reason they are given below. Read them carefully, asking yourself, how does each rule help Methodists keep God in first place?

THE GENERAL RULES OF METHODISM

In the latter end of the year 1739 eight or ten persons who appeared to be deeply convicted of sin, and earnestly groaning for redemption, came to Mr. Wesley in London. They desired, as did two or three more the next day, that we should spend some time with them in prayer, and advise them how to flee from the wrath to come, which they saw continually hanging over their heads. That he might have more time for this great work, he appointed a day when they might all come together, which from thenceforward they did every week, namely, on Thursday in the evening. To these, and as many more as desired to join with them (for their number increased daily), he gave those advices from time to time which he felt most needful for them, and they always concluded their meeting with prayer suited to their several necessities.

This was the rise of the United Society, first in Europe, and then in America. Such a society is no other than "a company of men having the form and seeking the power of godliness, united in order to pray together, to receive the word of exhortation, and to watch over one another in love, that they may help each other to work out their salvation."

That it may the more easily be discerned whether they are indeed working out their salvation, each society is divided into small companies, called classes, according to their respective places of abode. There are about twelve persons in a class, one of whom is styled the leader. It is his duty,

1. To see each person in his class once a week at least, in order: (1) to inquire how his soul prospers; (2) to advise, reprove, comfort, or exhort, as occasion may require; (3) to receive what he is willing to give toward the relief of the preachers, church, and poor.

2. To meet the ministers and the stewards of the society once a week, in order: (1) to inform the minister of any that are sick, or of any that are disorderly and will not be reproved; (2) to pay the stewards what he has received of his class in the week preceding.

There is only one condition previously required of those who desire admission into these societies—"a desire to flee from the wrath to come, and to be saved from their sins." *But wherever this is really fixed in the soul it will be shown by its fruits.*

It is therefore expected of all who continue therein that they shall continue to evidence their desire for salvation,

First: By doing no harm, by avoiding evil of every kind, especially that which is most generally practiced, such as:

Taking the name of God in vain.

The profaning of the day of the Lord, either by doing ordinary work therein or by buying or selling.

Drunkenness, buying or selling of spirituous liquors, or drinking them, unless in cases of extreme necessity.

Slaveholding; buying or selling slaves.

Fighting, quarreling, brawling, brother going to law with brother, returning evil for evil, or railing for railing; the using of many words in buying or selling.

The buying or selling goods that have not paid the duty.

The giving or taking of things on usury—that is, unlawful interest.

Uncharitable or unprofitable conversation; particularly speaking evil of magistrates or ministers.

Doing to others as we would not they should do unto us (Phil. 2: 12, 13).

Doing what we know is not for the glory of God, as:

The putting on of gold and costly apparel.

The taking of such diversions as cannot be used in the name of the Lord Jesus.

The singing of those songs, or reading those books, which do not tend to the knowledge or love of God.

Softness and needless self-indulgence.

Laying up treasure on Earth.

Borrowing without a probability of paying; or taking up goods without a probability of paying for them.

It is expected of all who continue in these societies that they shall continue to evidence their desire for salvation.

Second: By doing good; by being in every kind merciful after their power; as they have opportunity, doing good of every possible sort, and, as far as possible, to all men:

To their bodies, of the ability which God giveth, by giving food to the hungry, by clothing the naked, by visiting or helping them that are sick or in prison;

To their souls, by instructing, reproving, or exhorting all we have any intercourse with; trampling under foot that enthusiastic doctrine, that "we are not to do good unless our hearts be free to it."

By doing good, especially to them that are of the household of faith or groaning so to be; employing them preferably to others; buying one of another; helping each other in business; and so much the more because the world will love its own and them only.

By all possible diligence and frugality, that the Gospel be not blamed.

By running with patience the race which is set before them, denying themselves, and taking up their cross daily; submitting to bear the reproach of Christ, to be as the filth and offscouring of the world; and looking that men should say all manner of evil of them falsely, and for the Lord's sake.

It is expected of all who desire to continue in these

societies that they shall continue to evidence their desire of salvation.

Third: By attending upon all the ordinances of God; such are:

The public worship of God.

The ministry of the Word, either read or expounded.

The Supper of the Lord.

Family and private prayer.

Searching the Scriptures.

Fasting or abstinence.

These are the general rules of our societies; all of which we are taught of God to observe, even in His written Word, which is the only rule, and the sufficient rule, both of our faith and practice. And all these we know His Spirit writes on truly awakened hearts. If there be any among us who observes them not, who habitually breaks any of them, let it be known unto them who watch over that soul as they who must give an account. We will admonish him of the error of his ways. We will bear with him for a season. But, if then he repent not, he hath no more place among us. We have delivered our own souls.

These rules have long been in eclipse. Few Methodists know about them and rules of any sort seem archaic in the twentieth century with its emphasis on everybody doing his or her special "thing." Absolute standards of right and wrong no longer exist in many homes and churches. Most important, people's hearts and minds are undisciplined.

What has been the result? The influence of Methodists and Methodism has greatly declined. Texas evangelist Ed Robb tells the story of going to a small town, stopping at a service station and asking directions to the local Methodist church where he was supposed to preach. After hemming and hawing, the station attendant admitted didn't know where the church was. And he had li that town all his life.

Commented the evangelist, "This happen If anything was going on in the churc' know where it is."

That thousands of churches and millions of Methodists exist with little evident Christian influence in their communities is a sobering testimony. It reveals the deadness which is upon the Body of Christ. Getting rid of practical rules and spiritual disciplines, churches have thrown out the practical means of helping their people put God in first place. Pleasure, business, and standards of the world have taken over as number one.

Nothing exciting will happen until Methodists again resolve to give God His rightful place as Lord of life and Lord of the Church. This is what church renewal really means. It's all a matter of priorities, established in thousands of seemingly insignificant decisions as Christians either put God first or relegate Him to a place of lesser importance. The cumulative result of the millions of decisions by millions of people called Methodists greatly affects the society in which they live.

A challenge for you: The Methodist General Rules were drawn up over 200 years ago. Some conditions have obviously changed, such as the buying and selling of slaves. Read carefully through the rules. Change them to apply to today. Add any rules you think necessary for Methodists of the late twentieth century. If you add a rule, be sure you can find in the Bible a clear reason to justify this rule as a requirement for those wanting to put God first in their lives, in the church, and in the world.

QUESTIONS FOR DISCUSSION

1. *What causes people to set priorities in daily life? How many influences can you name?*

2. *Is the setting of priorities "a battleground known as hristian life"? Explain your opinion. Can you remem- any times of difficult decision? What part did God in arriving at your final decision?*

Why does God care about your priorities?

4. *Can you recall putting something ahead of God in your family? In your daily work? In your community? In the nation? What was the result?*

5. *What does the story of Mary and Martha (Luke 10) show about practical priorities? How did Jesus criticize the one who had worked to fix a nice dinner for Him?*

6. *Does your choice of friends reveal anything about your priorities?*

7. *Did Jesus establish radical, new priorities for His disciples and His church? What are some of them?*

8. *Why did early Methodists need the "General Rules"? How did these help Methodists to be "God's people"? Can someone be a Christian without rules? Explain.*

9. *How would you answer someone who said, "Christ sets people free from keeping rules"?*

10. *What is "spiritual discipline"? Is it separate from our daily tasks and responsibilities of job, family, and being good citizens?*

11. *Why were early Methodists often considered fanatics? Can you think of Christians today who are called the same thing? If you are not considered a fanatic about Jesus, what does this say about your faith and witness in the world?*

12. *From your reading of the "General Rules," what changes and additions would be needed if these were to be used by Methodists today?*

9

You Take Religion Seriously

"SOUR GODLINESS is the devil's religion," John Wesley once said. He meant religion without joy, devoid of that inner contentment welling up from within because Jesus is there, living His life through the Methodist.

But Wesley did not teach Methodists to be frivolous. To the contrary, serious seeking to know and do God's will has been, since the beginning, the characteristic of real Methodists. To be serious about your religion is an accurate outward sign of inward sincerity. Seriousness shows that a person has, in fact, heard the voice of God and is either moving toward new birth or is converted and "going on to perfection."

Seriousness . . . not perfectness. There is a big difference.

To demand perfectness would be to exclude all, for nobody is flawless in judgment and action. But to demand seriousness requires only what anyone can deliver—if that person really means business about his or her religion, if the Holy Spirit gives this seriousness as a gift of grace. Jesus said, "He who loves father or mother more than me is not worthy of me; and he who loves son or daughter more than me is not worthy of me; and he who does not take his cross and follow me is not worthy of me. He who finds his life will lose it, and he who loses his life for my sake will find it" (Matthew 10: 37-39, RSV). Serious religion indeed!

Jesus had a very practical way of testing people's religious seriousness. Once, in a crowd, Jesus was approached by a scribe. The man was full of newfound enthusiasm which Jesus seemed to have kindled. Ecstatic with joy, the man said, "Teacher, I will follow you wherever you go" (Matthew 8: 19, RSV).

Testing his seriousness, Jesus answered: "Foxes have holes, and birds of the air have nests; but the Son of man has nowhere to lay his head" (Matthew 8: 20, RSV). In effect, Jesus was saying, "Yes, come and follow me. But this will mean turning your back on the comforts of home and a settled life. If you are serious enough to pay this price you can be my disciple."

Another man felt a heart-tug to follow Jesus "all the way." But first, he explained, it would be necessary to take time to bury his father. Jesus saw this postponement as a symptom of divided loyalty. To make clear the seriousness of discipleship, Jesus said, "Follow me, and leave the dead to bury their own dead" (Matthew 8: 22). This was Jesus' way of saying that earthly ties—even so important as parents—must not be allowed to come before Him.

The historic Methodist seriousness about religion comes as a result of taking seriously the words of Jesus, of daring to think that these same "wonderful words of life" apply in our time, as in the first century.

A Methodist society was described by John Wesley as "a company of men [people] having the form and seeking

93

the power of godliness, united in order to pray together, to receive the word of exhortation, and to watch over one another in love, that they may help each other to work out their salvation."

All Methodists were either believers, or those in whom the Holy Spirit had stirred up a serious desire to "flee from the wrath to come which they saw continually hanging over their heads," as Wesley described it. Seriousness of seeking—or believing—was the only requirement needed to be and to remain a Methodist. If somebody ceased to be serious, they ceased to have reason for being a Methodist.

History shows instances where John Wesley, after careful examination to determine the seriousness of those in a Methodist society, removed scores or even several hundred people. Why? Because they lacked seriousness, and thus had ceased to be Methodists in spirit—even though their names were still on the membership roll. Each Methodist-in-good-standing was issued a quarterly ticket, so failure to reissue this ticket amounted to removal from membership in the society. Thus early Methodism was able to take quick action in removing members and also in restoring them on evidence of proper repentance and desire to again take seriously their Christian discipleship.

Wesley cared nothing about impressing the world with large membership statistics; instead, he cared about Methodists being an elite group of people who were serious about following Jesus and were therefore willing to accept the various personal and group Methodist disciplines to continue growing in usefulness to God and neighbor.

These disciplines were spelled out in the Methodist General Rules (see chapter eight). Since these rules are so important to an understanding of Methodists as serious Christians, please read them once more. After considering each one, ask yourself, "Would it show seriousness, if a

94

person did this (or avoided the prohibitions)?"

It is one thing to have a set of general rules printed in a book; it is something far more challenging to move them off the paper out into the life stream of a Christian group. Today, many churches are so like the world that anybody can do anything and still retain membership. The mere mention of "discipline" brings a negative reaction from many lay people and church officials alike: "It's not Christian to lay down hard and fast rules, to remove people from the church rolls!" Buttressed by this un-Biblical opinion, and by the desire to keep a large membership roll as the basis of prestige and per capita apportionment, mainline Methodists have practically abandoned congregational discipline. Either Methodists have matured since John Wesley's time making discipline unnecessary, or we have lost something vital from our Christian lives.

If we set aside the world's standards of permissiveness and see what Jesus had to say about discipline, we find our Lord sounding much like an early Methodist. "If your brother sins against you, go and tell him his fault, between you and him alone. If he listens to you, you have gained your brother. But if he does not listen, take one or two others along with you, that every word may be confirmed by the evidence of two or three witnesses. If he refuses to listen to them, tell it to the church; and if he refuses to listen even to the church, let him be to you as a Gentile [unbeliever] and a tax collector [flagrant sinner]. Truly, I say to you, whatever you bind on earth shall be bound in heaven, and whatever you loose on earth shall be loosed in heaven" (Matthew 18: 15-18, RSV).

To be "as a Gentile and a tax collector" meant to be excluded—excommunicated—with the purpose of bringing the erring one to repentance and restoration. This was Jesus' instruction for how to deal with those Christians who refuse to be reconciled: the guilty party must be cut off from the body of believers.

This seems harsh. Was Jesus wrong?

A doctor, detecting presence of gangrene on an arm, will cut off that infected arm in order to save the whole body. Sin unchecked can be to a group of Christians what gangrene is to the human body. Preservation and protection of Christ's Body, the church, is the first reason why Bible Christians recognize that strong discipline may become necessary.

God knows this too, as you can see in Acts 5. A husband and wife named Ananias and Sapphira belonged to the infant Jerusalem church. Some church members sold all their property and gave this to the Christian community as a sign of devotion to God and to their fellow Christians. Apparently this couple did the same thing—with one important difference. Secretly, they held back part of the proceeds for themselves. Their sin was not in keeping part of the cash, but in pretending to give all to God when they only gave part. This is hypocrisy, a familiar disease in the church then and now.

God's discipline was swift. In less than four hours God struck each of them dead—giving the infant church an unforgettable lesson of hypocrisy's deadly consequences. The Bible records, "And great fear came upon the whole church, and upon all who heard of these things" (Acts 5: 11). No wonder! It's a lesson still remembered by Bible Christians.

Read also the record of Paul's discipline of the Corinthian church member who was "living with his father's wife" (I Corinthians 5: 1b). Expulsion was the discipline, though later, in II Corinthians, Paul suggested this strong disciplinary measure had led the sinner to repent and to be restored to the church.

The Bible makes it very clear that discipline is necessary within the Christian community. To eliminate discipline is not "Christian" if you get from the Bible your understanding of what it means to be Christian. It is, instead, surrender to the spirit of a permissive age which lives by the motto "anything goes."

To be a true Methodist is to be a Bible Christian and hence, to practice discipline for the good of the church and the individual. In the book, *Church Membership in the Methodist Tradition,* Professor Frederick A. Norwood writes of historic Methodism: "Members were expected to 'watch over each other in love.' Time and again we return to this underlying theme of the priesthood of all believers. This is the leaven in the lump of discipline. All the strictness of the rules, all the urgency of the inquiry, all the soberness of reproof, all the tyranny of regimentation, all the grimness of expulsion, must be seen and understood in the light of the saving grace of brotherly love, mutual concern, self-giving witness to faith in Christ. When this fellowship is gone, then discipline becomes petty, hateful, carping, and destructive. Only a church in which each ministers to all can abide the rigor of the original Wesleyan discipline."

Christian discipline has two branches. One is the branch of corporate discipline within the community of believers. The other, closely related of course, is God disciplining His children individually. This, too, is a foreign thought to many of today's church members. God has been given the modern image of a tolerant Father who, like many human fathers, indulges his children endlessly without ever a thought of punishment. Thus the Bible's God has been melted down to conform to the mood and spirit of this permissive age.

But Methodists, being Bible Christians, know that divine punishment is a necessary dimension of the Father's love. " 'My son, don't be angry when the Lord punishes you. Don't be discouraged when he has to show you where you are wrong. For when he punishes you, it proves that he loves you. When he whips you it proves you are really his child.' Let God train you, for he is doing what any loving father does for his children. Whoever heard of a son who was never corrected? If God doesn't punish you when you need it, as other fathers punish their sons, then it means that you aren't really God's son at all—that you don't really belong in his family. Since we respect our fathers here on earth, though they punish us, should we not all the more cheerfully submit to God's training so that we can begin really to live? Our earthly fathers trained us for a few brief years, doing the best for us that they knew how, but God's correction is always right and for our best good, that we may share his holiness. Being punished isn't enjoyable while it is happening —it hurts! But afterwards we can see the result, a quiet growth in grace and character" (Hebrews 12: 5b-11, LB).

This basic Bible truth is reflected in Wesley's *Character of a Methodist*: ". . . The Methodist gives thanks to God at all times, and in all circumstances. For the Methodist knows that God expects His children to be always grateful.

"The Methodist receives every happening cheerfully, declaring, 'Good is the will of the Lord.' Whether the Lord gives or takes away, the Methodist blesses the name of the Lord.

"Another characteristic of the Methodist: he has learned to be content, whether he has much or little. When humiliation comes, the Methodist accepts it gladly as the Father's will. When prosperity and good fortune come, the Methodist likewise gives God the credit. The Methodist accepts all circumstances gladly, knowing that these are God's doing, intended for his ultimate good . . ."

Such was the faith of Job: "The Lord gave, and the Lord has taken away; blessed be the name of the Lord" (Job 1: 21b).

Such was the psalmist's faith: "I will bless the Lord at all times; his praise shall continually be in my mouth" (Psalm 34: 1).

Such was Jesus' faith: "Nevertheless not my will, but thine, be done" (Luke 22: 42b).

Such was Paul's faith: "We know that in everything God works for good with those who love him, who are called according to his purpose" (Romans 8: 28).

Such was Peter's faith: "In this [the assurance of salvation] you rejoice, though now for a little while you may have to suffer various trials, so that the genuineness of your faith, more precious than gold which though perishable is tested by fire, may redound to praise and glory and honor at the revelation of Jesus Christ" (I Peter 1: 6, 7, RSV).

Such was James' faith: "Count it all joy, my brethren, when you meet various trials, for you know that the testing of your faith produces steadfastness" (James 1: 2, 3).

Such is the faith of every true Methodist, expressed in this contemporary hymn:

"Father, I trust in You
    To do what's always best
Though I can't really understand
    Why I am put to the test.

Why must I stumble so?
    Why must my faith be dim?
Sometimes it seems as if my Lord
    Would let me abandon Him.

Father, I hear Your word
    Speaking again to me,
"Count it all joy," when trouble comes
    It deepens humility.

Father, I trust in You
    Chastise me as You will.
I know Your wrath, it comes from love
    To make me stronger still.
                    —*Charles W. Keysor*

QUESTIONS FOR DISCUSSION

1. *What does the word "discipline" mean?*

2. *Is "discipline" ever contrary to the Christian ideal of perfect love? Explain your opinion.*

3. *What is the relationship between discipline and love?*

4. *With discipline like the "General Rules," how did early Methodism appeal to so many people? Today, what might happen if a church should insist that its members follow such rules?*

5. *The Bible says children need discipline and if parents fail to provide discipline they do not really love their children. Comment on this in light of popular theories on child-rearing which make it wrong for parents to say "no." What is your opinion of this teaching, based on your own experiences with family relationships?*

6. *What makes the difference between discipline that is cruel or self-righteous and discipline which has in it the love of Jesus?*

7. *Explain the harsh discipline God meted out to Ananias and Sapphira as reported in Acts, chapter five. Do you think the double death penalty was justified?*

8. *In a local church, what can make discipline difficult?*

9. *Would your church be different if Jesus's rule for settling differences among believers was taken literally? Would you be in favor of doing this? Have you ever tried this way of dealing with a Christian who has sinned against you? What happened?*

10. *Comment on John Wesley's expression "sour godliness is the devil's religion." Have you ever seen someone afflicted with "sour godliness"? What effect did this person have on others?*

11. *What is the difference between making seriousness and being "perfect" the standard for belonging to a church? Why did Wesley make seriousness the first requirement for being and remaining a Methodist?*

12. *What might your church be like if, in historic Methodist fashion, only serious Christians or seekers were permitted to be members?*

10

You Are a Part of Christ's Body

CAN YOU BE A CHRISTIAN all by yourself?

Many people think they can. The idea of religious individualism—"just Jesus and me"—is deeply enshrined in American folk-religion. Some preachers, evangelists, teachers, and hymn writers (plus the naturally individualistic nature of people) combine to make private religion a popular dogma.

I encountered this view of religion often during the nine years I was a United Methodist pastor.

Once, when I was visiting in the home of an inactive member, a mother asked me to baptize her daughter. She wanted a family-only "christening" in her home. It should be done right after supper so as not to interfere with evening television programs.

I replied that baptism is a sacrament of the church of Jesus Christ. It could not, I explained, be sandwiched between dinner and Gunsmoke. I explained that I baptized privately only in extreme emergencies, that to perform a baptism without God's people would be like performing a marriage without the bride. Together, the church needs to praise God for each new dedication of life. Together, the community of Jesus' people needs to lift its voice in corporate praise for what baptism represents. Together, God's people need to intercede with the Heavenly Father, asking that He pour out in the home divine love, power, and kind perseverance—without which baptismal promises cannot be kept. Together, mother, dad, and the children need to be part of the Body of Christ, where they can grow together along with other disciples in the grace and knowledge of the Lord Jesus Christ.

The lady listened, becoming angrier by the minute. Finally she burst out, "What does the church have to do with the baptism of my daughter?"

The visit ended with her being adamant, and with my suggesting that she could probably find some other preacher who would baptize according to the dictates of her private religion. (She did!)

My richest pastoral memories concern those times when I found a close unity in faith and service with other believers. In such high and holy moments, I believe that by God's grace we were being the church as He showed it to be in the New Testament and in the historic Methodism of John and Charles Wesley. I remember spending the late afternoon in a hospital waiting room with one of our members. His wife was undergoing surgery for cancer and our vigil lasted several hours. When the surgeon appeared he said, "We have done all we can. I think we got all the cancerous tissue but only time will tell."

Afterward, I talked and prayed with the husband. I reminded him that the church exists, in times of trial, so we can "help carry one another's burdens, and in this way you will obey the law of Christ" (Galatians 6: 2, TEV). Then I opened my Bible and read, "Is any among you sick? Let him call for the elders of the church, and let them pray over him, anointing him with oil in the name of the Lord; and the prayer of faith will save the sick man, and the Lord will raise him up; and if he has committed sins, he will be forgiven" (James 5: 14, 15, RSV).

"Blackie," I asked, "would you like us to come tonight and pray with Juanita?"

That evening I returned with two laymen whom the Holy Spirit had led me to invite. Both were nervous. They had often read this passage of Scripture, but had never literally carried it out.

" 'Nita," I said, "the church has come to pray with you and for you."

Through the pain, she smiled and grasped my hand powerfully.

I touched her head with olive oil, so richly symbolic of God's anointing. Then the three of us, all ministers, laid our hands upon the sick woman's head, symbolizing those far greater hands of love which were, in that instant, reaching from Heaven (through our hands) to work a miracle of healing and cleansing. We prayed believing that it was ordained of God and commanded in His Word. We prayed trusting that God would act according to His promise.

We were the church, the five of us in that hospital room. Jesus was there and He brought healing.

This, I believe, is the church at its best—believers doing God's will in unity, love, trust, and utter helplessness, knit together by a mysterious and supernatural bond which defies human programing and explanation.

Love divine, all loves excelling!
    Joy of Heaven to Earth come down.
Fix in us Thy humble dwelling
    All Thy faithful mercies crown.
Jesus, Thou art all compassion
    Pure unbounded love Thou art

Visit us with Thy salvation
  Enter every trembling heart.—*Charles Wesley*

John Wesley knew that no one could remain a Christian all alone. "The spirit indeed is willing, but the flesh is weak" (Mark 14: 38). His own long struggle to find God (chapter one) and then his years as a soldier of Christ convinced Wesley of the need to "be alert, be on watch! Your enemy, the Devil, roams around like a roaring lion, looking for someone to devour. Be firm in your faith and resist him" (I Peter 5: 8, 9a, TEV).

Wesley also knew that a Christian person is something like a coal in your charcoal barbecue stove. Take that coal out of the fire and set it on the ground. Soon the coal will be cold and gray. It needs to be sustained by the fire of others close around it. Together they burn; singly they die.

Take a Christian out of regular contact with corporate praise, worship, sacraments, and hearing the Gospel with true believers and that transplanted Christian will grow cold spiritually. This happens because God's Spirit is present in a special way "where two or three come together in my [Jesus] name" because "I am there with them" (Matthew 18: 20, TEV). Jesus comes individually, of course, to save, to convict or comfort, and to provide the mountaintop experiences known to all believers.

But these cannot substitute for our regular experiencing of our Lord's unique ministry that happens whenever believers gather in His name under the moving of His Spirit. A woman who had long been a church refugee got tired of trying to face life alone. Timidly, she came to worship one Sunday morning.

"It was as if God reached out and put His arms around me," she declared afterward, in breathless amazement. It was not the sermon, nor the choir, nor the order of worship, nor the friendly people which produced this effect. It was Jesus, present in Resurrection power among those who loved Him, who had assembled to worship Him, to hear His Word preached under the direction of the Holy Spirit.

From the Bible and from personal experience, John Wesley knew that true Christian faith must be corporate. To provide a sort of incubator where faith could grow among the people called Methodist, he organized a Society wherever Methodist preaching roused spiritual hunger and drew seekers to Christ. These people were divided into "classes," numbering ten or twelve each. Wesley appointed a "class leader," a relatively mature Christian who had demonstrated spiritual insight and potential for leadership to be in charge of each group.

Every week this leader personally visited every class member. "How's it going," the class leader would ask, "with you and the Lord? With your family? With you and other Methodists? With your friends and neighbors?"

Relationships were seen as all-important, for Bible faith always shows itself in relationship between the believer, God, and other people. Methodists have never wasted much time with religious ideas that did not directly affect relationships. Perhaps that is why Methodists have been called "God's most practical people."

The Biblical blend of faith and practical concern multiplies in the close, personal, Spirit-filled atmosphere of a small group of believers. That was the secret of the Methodist classes. They were the spiritual powerhouses, the incubators of practical love and concern tested in the arena of daily living.

Sometimes the class leader, in making his weekly personal visits, found a class member in need or in trouble. Other class members were quickly summoned for help with prayer, food, money, clothes or assistance in finding a job. And so the Methodist classes gave Christians a chance to look after one another. "Suppose there are brothers or sisters [fellow Christians] who need clothes and don't have enough to eat. What good is there in your saying to them, 'God bless you! Keep warm and eat well!'—if you don't give them the necessities of life?" (James 2: 15, 16, TEV).

The classes offered early Methodists a laboratory for living out the Gospel. By contrast, the impersonality of so much modern church life kills faith and stifles love. Large, cold, professionally run churches do not provide much laboratory experience in caring, in "doing the faith." How can Christian intimacy be achieved when people see one another only weekly; and then only one third of the congregation together for a brief church school class and worship service? People can be members of the same church for years and never get close enough to experience what is so beautifully expressed in this familiar hymn:

"We share each other's woes
　Our mutual burdens bear,
And often for each other flows
　The sympathizing tear."—*John Fawcett*

Attending the weekly class was a must. Methodist leaders knew it was a matter of spiritual survival. That is why the early Methodist discipline was so strong: to serve as a warning-in-love to those who were playing spiritual Russian roulette by losing touch with their brothers and sisters in Christ.

When the class met, the leader took an offering (in true Methodist style!). They sang some hymns, especially the beloved ones by Charles Wesley. One of these catches perfectly the closeness of Methodist class-meeting fellowship in the Lord:

And we are yet alive,
　And see each other's face?
Glory and thanks to Jesus give
　For His almighty grace.
What troubles have we seen
　What mighty conflicts passed
Fightings without and fears within

Since we assembled last!
Yet out of all the Lord
  Has brought us by His love
And still He doth His help afford
  And hides our life above.
Then let us make our boast
  Of His redeeming power
Which saves us to the uttermost
  'Till we can sin no more.

There was praying. The leader went around the class and asked each person to testify to some victory in the Lord, or, if need be, to lift before the group some special struggle, weakness, or temptation. Then the group would minister to that individual. There was, of course, study of the Bible, adjournment, and the lingering which is the precious afterglow when Christ has been present with Christian people, and His love is felt among them.

Reading these things should cause Methodists to realize the great difference between Methodism today and at the beginning. The widespread growth of "sharing groups" and other groups for prayer and discussion are an effort to recapture the intense closeness known and treasured by our Methodist forefathers. Today's Methodists are weary of depersonalized church life where the "sympathizing tear" is rarely shed (we are too busy, too dignified).

The condition of Methodism today has much in common with the Anglican Church in Wesley's day. Then as now, lethargy and spiritual deadness seemed to prevail. Over 200 years ago, God led John Wesley to stay within the institutional church—but to survive by creating within it living cells comprised of what the New Testament says Christ's churches ought to be. Wesley expected Methodists to be agents of renewal and reformation—to move out as spiritually radioactive particles and radiate for Christ the dead institutional church of that day.

This strategy could work today.

Suppose people hungering after more vital Christianity

would organize, right in their living rooms, Wesley-type classes.

Suppose the people agreed among themselves and God —to put their class meeting first, ahead of all other obligations.

Suppose a godly leader was chosen and given the task of being the shepherd—of personally visiting each week each class member.

Suppose other class members loved one another enough to set aside anything if a brother or sister had an emergency.

Suppose each week they sang together, prayed together, shared their time, their affections, their talents and their money to make the Kingdom real—at least in the lives of those "called out ones."

Suppose there were intense intercessory prayer, good works abounding, and the Spirit of Jesus bringing a holy radiance to this fellowship.

Suppose nominal church members were moved to say in amazement, "See how these Christians love one another!"

Might God be waiting for such a commitment on the part of a few real Methodists? Might this be the trigger to begin a revival that would be felt around the world? It happened in John Wesley's day, and the spiritual laws which he followed have never been repealed.

Suppose . . .

QUESTIONS FOR DISCUSSION

1. *Do you agree that a person can't be a Christian alone? That apart from regular contact with believers, one's spiritual life will be like a coal taken out of the fire? Explain.*

2. *Can you think of some things that make it hard to be a "lone Christian"?*

3. *What causes some church members to think they don't need the church? Is this ever justified?*

4. *What miracle happens when a group of Christians gather to celebrate the glory of God in the Resurrection power of Jesus Christ? Could the same thing happen in the experience of people who "go to church" by watching televised religious programs?*

5. *This chapter contained one example of private faith and another about the togetherness of the church in times of personal crisis. Can you recall these examples? Can you explain what they show about the church? Life?*

6. *The Methodist classes were described as "incubators" and also as "laboratories." How do these words describe a group of believers?*

7. *Why did John Wesley organize Methodist societies into classes?*

8. *With as much detail as possible describe how a class was set up and how it operated.*

9. *From what you have read about Methodist classes, do you think they might be set up today within Methodist congregations? What could be the benefits? What might be the dangers?*

10. *Explain John Wesley's idea that Methodists should serve God as "seasoning" for the established church. What meaning does this have today?*

11. *What parallel can you see between the classes of early Methodism and the prayer and sharing groups so common today? Are they the same thing?*

12. *What can be done to remedy the impersonal nature of much church life today? Is it caused by ministers? By laymen?*

11

Your God Is Big Enough

JOHN WESLEY WAS PREACHING to a crowd in Drewbury, England. Through the throng came an angry man who hated the church and Christians. He pushed his way up to where the Methodist leader was preaching and he slapped John Wesley in the face.

The shocked crowd watched to see what would happen.

Those standing close to Wesley saw tears in his eyes. Then the famous preacher turned his other cheek toward his attacker.

"Instead of smiting it," one report said, "the attacker was overawed and immediately hid himself among the crowd. From this circumstance, instead of being an enemy of Mr. Wesley, he became an admirer and a great friend of Methodism."

Methodists have a great God! Great enough to give a man the strength to return good for evil.

So it has been through over 200 years of Methodist

history. One of the outstanding marks of a real Methodist is faith in a mighty and all-powerful God.

One of the early Methodists in America was Freeborn Garrettson, a Marylander. Traveling by horse and foot, he preached his way through the Carolinas, Pennsylvania, Delaware, New Jersey, and up North into Nova Scotia. Garrettson's father died, and the preacher inherted an estate, including some slaves. Along with many other people in Maryland at that time, Garrettson had never thought about the morality of white men keeping black men in bondage.

In *The Story of American Methodism,* the authors report, "he began to feel his preaching growing feeble. He had no inkling what the matter could be, but he knew something was wrong, and began to agonize over it.

"At last he called his whole family together for a session of common prayer. As he stood before them, about to announce a hymn, he seemed to hear an inner voice saying, 'It is not right for you to keep your fellow creatures in bondage; you must let the oppressed go free.'

"Without a moment's hesitation he told the slaves that they were free men, and then, in his own words, 'I was now at liberty to proceed in worship. Had I the tongue of an angel, I could not fully describe what I felt. All my dejection, and that melancholy gloom which preyed upon me, vanished in a moment, and a divine sweetness ran through my whole frame.' "

Methodists have a great God! Great enough to break down established social wrongs and cause a man to feel guilt and then freedom, when he treats other people the way he would like them to treat him.

Bishop Francis Asbury was the man whom God used to lay Methodism's real foundations in America. It is said that during his 45 years of ministry, while preaching the

Gospel and supervising the expanding network of Methodist circuits and annual conferences, he rode on horseback more than 250,000 miles, mostly over wilderness trails.

His journal contains this record: "On Saturday I found that among my other trials I had taken an uncomfortable skin disease. Considering the filthy houses and filthy beds I have met with in coming from Kentucky, it is perhaps strange that I did not catch it 20 times. I do not see that there is any securing against it, but by sleeping in my brimstone shirt."

Methodists have a great God! Great enough to win the loyalty of a talented leader, cause him to sacrifice the comforts most men prize, and spend his life as a lonesome traveler.

The year is 1833. The American Colonization Society had worked since 1820 to establish in West Africa a nation for freed slaves. It was named Liberia. Methodist settlers there had sent back word to America: "We need missionaries!" Melville Cox volunteered, knowing he would be going into what had been called "the white man's graveyard" where tropical fevers and hot climate are often lethal. But God called, so Cox went.

Cox lived only four months, and in that short time he laid the foundations for countless Methodist missionaries who were to follow. On his tombstone are the words of his dying missionary challenge to Methodists back in America: "Though a thousand fall, let not Africa be given up!"

Methodists have a great God! Great enough to command such loyalty that a man, loving God more than life itself, will die for the Kingdom's sake.

"Big Jim" was an engineer on the railroad near Chicago. He had grown up during the Great Depression in rural Mississippi, where preachers sometimes shouted for hours, and where poor boys slipped into church in order to enjoy the supper afterward.

Jim had been a railroad bum, a policeman, an odd-jobber. World War II carried him around the world on merchant ships. He saw men die. He watched ships loaded with ammunition disappear in the blinding flash of a torpedo hit.

Drinking and gambling followed the war. God gave Jim a lovely family, but he regarded Sunday as only a respite from the round of taverns and a chance for his hangovers to ease off.

Near Jim's house was a Methodist church, small, unpretentious, old. The children went there to Sunday school and they begged their dad to come, too.

One Sunday morning Jim's oldest daughter said, "If you don't go to church Dad, why should I?"

Stung by parental guilt, Jim combed his hair, put on his suit and came to church with his daughter.

He came the next Sunday and the next. People weren't especially cordial, and the preacher didn't pay much attention to Jim. But God was speaking to him. The Gospel he heard stirred echoes of childhood and brought deep conviction over all the empty, wasted years. One day in the church, Jim gave his life to Jesus. Christ came into his life and his home. Jim and his wife joined the church and eventually Jim became lay leader of the congregation. When he led the people in prayer, worship, and testimony, God spoke through him in a direct and beautiful way.

Methodists have a great God! He is ready, willing and able to save to the uttermost anyone who comes to him.

I could tell from the evasiveness of the doctors that something was wrong.

"We don't have a conclusive report yet," the surgeons said. "We are having some additional lab work done."

As a pastor, I had been around doctors and hospitals enough to know what it meant. But this time the patient was my own wife. She had gone for exploratory surgery, and now, afterward, we waited.

We had prayed for her healing. The church had prayed. And now we could only wait for the doctor's verdict. Strangely, neither of us felt any fear. We felt, instead, a sense of calm. We knew God was in charge and we trusted Him.

Finally, we talked with the doctors. They were puzzled. "When we saw the tumor," they said, "we were sure it was an advanced malignancy, probably terminal. But the first lab test showed no malignancy. Two more tests by other labs showed the same thing. There is no cancer. We don't understand this."

We knew what had happened. The Great Physician had touched my wife with healing beyond the understanding of medical science.

Methodists have a great God! Great enough to heal the body and still the soul in life's deepest crises.

In the language of the theologians, this is known as the "sovereignty of God." It means that God is all-wise, all-powerful, all-loving and that His will—sometimes inscrutable—is always directed to the highest good for those who love Him and are called according to His purpose (Romans 8: 28).

This was the God whom John Wesley worshiped and served. Bowing before His Divine Majesty, Wesley was able to stand before the world, tall, strong, fearless, and effective. Here we find a secret shared by every truly effective Christian: Faith in an all-powerful God sets you free from bondage to all who would control you. "If God is for us, who can be against us? He did not even keep back his own Son, but offered him for us all! He gave us his Son—will he not also freely give us all things? Who

114

will accuse God's chosen people? God himself declares them not guilty! Can anyone, then, condemn them? Christ Jesus is the one who died, or rather, who was raised to life and is at the right side of God. He pleads with God for us!" (Romans 8: 31b-34, TEV).

Immerse yourself in the Bible. Read it from Genesis to Revelation and you will read about "a God of miracles" who "hung the world in space." But because the Bible has been so widely disregarded, many people think of God as being limited. This is why the English Bible scholar, J. B. Phillips, wrote the book, *Your God Is Too Small!*

Perhaps Methodists are not changing the world because our God is too small. We have allowed learned "higher critics" to strip the Scriptures of the truth, "God is great." By denying miracles and "demythologizing," the church has sometimes reduced God to the size of a mere man. The well known humanist, the late Episcopal Bishop James Pike, wrote in a magazine article shortly before his death about the *"deity* of man."

Such an idea is blasphemy to anyone who knows personally the God and Father of our Lord Jesus Christ.

Ask the woman cured of cancer.

Ask "Big Jim."

And when you get to Heaven, ask Bishop Asbury, Melville Cox, Freeborn Garrettson, and John Wesley. In fact, ask the multitudes who are even now singing God's praises around the Eternal Throne. They may reply by using these words of praise to God by Charles Wesley:

Thy ceaseless, unexhausted love
  Unmerited and free
Delights our evil to remove
  And help our misery.

Thou waitest to be gracious still
  Thou dost with sinners bear
That, saved, we may Thy goodness
  And all Thy grace declare.

Thy goodness and Thy truth to me
　To every soul abound
A vast unfathomable sea
　Where all our thoughts are drowned.

Its streams the whole creation reach
　So plenteous is the store
Enough for all, enough for each
　Enough for evermore.

Faithful, O Lord, Thy mercies are
　The rock that cannot move.
A thousand promises declare
　Thy constancy of love.

Throughout the universe it reigns
　Unalterably sure
And while the truth of God remains
　Thy goodness must endure.

QUESTIONS FOR DISCUSSION

1. *Have you ever had a problem that even God could not, or would not, solve?*

2. *Where should Christians get their measurement of God?*

3. *Is it blasphemy to say that mankind has "deity"? Do you suppose that many church members really think this, perhaps without saying it openly?*

4. *Consider your relationship with God. What things have happened that make you want to sing, "How Great Thou Art"?*

5. *Why has the Swedish hymn, "How Great Thou Art," become so popular? Why do some people dislike this hymn?*

6. *How would you explain to a child the greatness of God?*

7. *Is there any situation which God is not able to control? What about wars, earthquakes, and poverty?*

8. *What is meant by the "sovereignty of God"?*

9. *Why does appreciation for God's greatness bring a sense of strength and security to believers?*

10. *What are some Bible verses that make clear the supreme greatness of God?*

11. *As a subject of meditation, reflect on Charles Wes-*

ley's hymn of praise at the end of this chapter. Think carefully about each line and stanza. Can you honestly say, "This is my faith as well as Charles Wesley's"?

12. What is the best way to help other people realize and appreciate God's greatness?

12

You Have Christ's Character

THE ORIGINAL METHODIST wrote many things during his long and busy life. Nothing from his pen so clearly and completely summarizes Methodism as the pamphlet, *Character of a Methodist.*

Unfortunately, few people have seen this because it is long out of print, a great Methodist treasure lost.

A modern language paraphrase of this pamphlet is given below. Without changing the meaning of Wesley, the work has been put into today's language so that John Wesley can speak directly to you.

Read through this chapter swiftly for an overview. Then go back and carefully explore each sentence. You can read it devotionally. Or you may want to gather together some people who are serious about Bible Christianity. Many profitable weeks of group study can be spent with *Character of a Methodist.**

"The distinguishing marks of a Methodist are not his

*The Character of a Methodist by John Wesley Paraphrased in Today's Language," used by permission of the Forum for Scriptural Christianity within the United Methodist Church, Inc., who first published this paraphrase in Good News Magazine, 1967.

opinions of any sort . . . his accepting this or that scheme of religion . . . his embracing any particular set of notions . . . or mouthing the judgments of one man or another. All these are quite wide of the point.

"Therefore, whoever imagines that a Methodist is a man of such and such opinion is sadly ignorant. We do believe that 'all Scripture is given by inspiration of God.' This distinguishes us from all non-Christians. We believe that the written Word of God is the only and sufficient rule both of Christian faith and practice in our lives. And this distinguishes us from the Roman Catholic Church.

"We believe that Christ is the eternal, supreme God. This distinguishes us from those who consider Jesus Christ to be less than deity.

"But as to all opinions which do not strike at the root of Christianity, we think and let think. This means that whether or not these secondary opinions are right or wrong, they are not the distinguishing marks of a Methodist.

"Neither are words or phrases of any sort. For our religion does not depend on any particular way of speaking. We do not rely upon any quaint or uncommon expressions. The most obvious, easy words which convey the truth most effectively—these we Methodists prefer, in daily speech and when we speak about the things of God. We never depart from the most common, ordinary way of speaking—unless it be to express Scriptural truths in the words of Scripture. And we don't suppose any Christian will condemn us for this.

"We don't put on airs by repeating certain Scriptural expressions—unless these are used by the inspired writers themselves.

"Our religion does not consist of doing only those things which God has not forbidden. It is not a matter of our clothes or the way we walk; whether our heads are covered; or in abstaining from marriage or from food and drink. (All these things can be good if they are received gratefully and used reverently as blessings given to us by God.) Nobody who knows the truth will try to identify a Methodist by any of these outward appearances.

"Nor is a Methodist identified because he bases his religion on any particular *part* of God's truth. By 'salvation' the Methodist means holiness of heart and life. This springs from true faith, and nothing else. Can even a nominal Christian deny this?

"This concept of faith does not mean we are declaring God's law to be void through faith. God forbid such a perverted conclusion. Instead, we Methodists believe that faith is the means by which God's law is established.

"There are too many people who make a religion out of (1) doing no harm, or (2) doing good (and often these two together). God knows, we Methodists do not fall into this mistaken way of defining our Christianity. Experience proves that many people struggle vainly for a long, long time with this false idea of religion consisting of good works (or no bad works). In the end, these deluded people have no religion at all; they are no better off than when they started.

"Then what is the distinguishing mark of a Methodist? Who is a Methodist?

"A Methodist is a person who has the love of God in his heart. This is a gift of God's Holy Spirit. And the same Spirit causes a Methodist to love the Lord his God with all his heart, with all his soul, with all his mind, with all his strength.

"God is the joy of a Methodist's heart; the desire of his soul, which cries out constantly, 'Whom have I in Heaven but You, Lord? There is nothing on Earth that I desire but You, my God and my All. You are the strength of my life. You, Lord, are all that I need.'

"Naturally, the Methodist is happy in God. Yes, he is always happy because the Methodist has within him that

'well of water' which Christ promised. It floods up to overflowing, bringing glorious assurance of the life that never
ends. Therefore, the Methodist is a person in whom God's
peace and joy are constantly evident. The Methodist does
not fear God's wrath for himself. Perfect love has ban-
ished fear of God's punishment from the Methodist's
heart. For this reason, he is able to rejoice evermore. He
does not rejoice in himself or in his achievements. Instead
the Methodist rejoices in God, who is his Lord and Savior.

"The Methodist acknowledges God as his Father. Why?
Because the Methodist has from Jesus Christ the power
to become a glad and grateful son of the Father.

"The Methodist is one who realizes that he belongs to
God instead of to Satan. This is redemption. It is possible
only because Jesus gave His life on the Cross. He shed
His blood to make atonement for the sins of all who believe in Him. The Methodist trusts in Christ alone for his
salvation. The Methodist knows that the blood of Jesus
Christ has cleansed him from all sin. Through Christ and
Christ alone the Methodist has received forgiveness for
his sins.

"The Methodist never forgets this. And the Methodist
shudders as he considers the eternal punishment from
which he has been delivered by Jesus Christ. The Methodist gives thanks that God loved him enough to spare
him—to blot out his transgressions and iniquities . . . to
atone for them with the shed blood and broken body of
His beloved Son.

"Having personally experienced deliverance from God's
wrath, the Methodist cannot help rejoicing. He rejoices
every time he thinks of his narrow escape from eternal
destruction. He rejoices that by God's kindness he, a sinner, has been placed in a new and right relationship with
His creator. This miracle has been accomplished through
Jesus Christ, the Methodist's beloved Savior.

"Whoever thus believes, experiences the assurance of God's love and forgiveness. This clear and certain inner recognition is witness that the Methodist is a son of God by faith. This truth is made known to the Methodist as God sends His own Spirit to bear witness deep within the mind and soul of the Methodist, enabling him to cry out 'Father, my Father!' This is the inner witness of God's Holy Spirit, testifying to the Methodist of his adoption into God's own family.

"The Methodist rejoices because he looks forward confidently to seeing the glory of Christ fully revealed one day. This expectation is a source of great joy, and the Methodist exalts, 'Blessed be the God and Father of our Lord Jesus Christ! According to the Father's abundant mercy He caused me to be reborn so I can enjoy this eternal hope which never fades or tarnishes. This is an inheritance of faith. It cannot be stolen, lost, or destroyed in any way. It is a pure and permanent hope. God has reserved its fulfillment in eternity for me.'

"Having this great hope, the Methodist gives thanks to God at all times, and in all circumstances. For the Methodist knows that God expects His children to be always grateful.

"The Methodist receives every happening cheerfully, declaring, 'Good is the will of the Lord.' Whether the Lord gives or takes away, the Methodist blesses the name of the Lord.

"Another characteristic of the Methodist: he has learned to be content, whether he has much or little. When humiliation comes, the Methodist accepts this gladly as the Father's will. When prosperity and good fortune come, the Methodist likewise gives God the credit. The Methodist accepts all circumstances gladly, knowing that these are God's doing, intended for his ultimate good.

"Whether he is in leisure or suffering pain, whether he is sick or in good health, whether he lives or dies, the

Methodist gives thanks to God from the very depths of his heart. For the Methodist trusts that God's ways are always good, that every wonderful and perfect gift comes from God, into whose providential hand the Methodist has committed his body and soul.

"The Methodist knows no paralyzing frustration and anxiety. For the Methodist has thankfully cast his every care upon God, never failing to let God know all about his needs and problems.

"The Methodist never stops praying. It is second nature for him to pray and not to be discouraged. This does not mean that the Methodist is always praying in a church building. (Though it goes without saying that the Methodist misses no opportunity for public worship.) The Methodist is often on his knees in humility before God, but he does not spend all his time in contemplation.

"Nor does the Methodist try to beat God's ears with many words. For the Holy Spirit speaks to God on behalf of the Methodist, expressing his innermost hopes and longings that human words cannot articulate. This alone is true prayer; the language of the heart which overflows with joy, sometimes is best expressed in holy silence before God.

"The Methodist's whole self is tuned to God's will— at all times, and in all circumstances. Nothing can sever the bond that unites the Methodist and his God. This constant sense of closeness cannot be broken by business, leisure, or conversation. This closeness to God is the true sign of the Methodist's love for his Creator and Redeemer. Therefore, the Methodist walks with God, being constantly aware of Him who is invisible and immortal.

"Inscribed indelibly on the Methodist's heart is the truth that 'he who loves God loves his brother also.' This means that the Methodist cares about his neighbor as much as he cares about himself.

"His heart is full of love for everyone. This love does

not stop with the Methodist's personal acquaintances; it encircles all mankind. Even those who hate the Methodist receive love in return. For like Jesus, the Methodist loves his enemies. And the Methodist loves even God's enemies, the evil and the unthankful. If the Methodist cannot possibly do good to his enemies, still the Methodist prays for those who trouble and insult him. This is what it means to be 'pure in heart.'

"The Methodist can experience this purity because God has cleansed the Methodist's heart, washing away all urge for revenge, all envy, all wrath, all desire for harming another person. Every unkind inclination is gone, every evil lust and desire, too. Pride has been purged out of the Methodist mind and heart. Gone also is haughtiness which always causes friction between people.

"In place of these 'human' weaknesses, the Methodist has taken the character of Christ. This is evident in a true Methodist's meekness, patience in the face of frustration, absence of pride, honest estimate of his own strengths and weaknesses.

"If anybody causes him trouble, embarrassment or discomfort, the Methodist can forgive. Because God, for the sake of Christ, has forgiven the Methodist for his sins. All of this means that the Methodist never has reason to quarrel or fight with anybody, regardless of how great the provocation. And why should the Methodist fight? Nobody can take from him the things he considers most important: God and the things of God. The Methodist is immune to conflict because he has crucified his 'old self' which used to be directed by the desires and standards of the lower nature.

"There is one great desire which motivates the Methodist: to do not his own will, but God's. The Methodist's single intention is to please God. This absorption with God fills the Methodist's life with radiance, joy, peace at all times. Because the Methodist is focused on God to the exclusion of all else, the light which is God fills the Methodist's whole being. Thus he is a child of Light.

"So God reigns alone and supreme within the Methodist. No motion of the Methodist's mind is out of tune with God's gracious, sovereign will. A Methodist's every thought and action points to the Lord.

"Anybody can identify a tree by its fruits. So also the Methodist is known because his life bears the fruit for God: Keeping all the commandments from the greatest to the very least. The Methodist conscience is clear before God. Whatever God forbids, that the Methodist avoids. Whatever God has commanded, the Methodist does, whether this involves joy or grief, ease or great difficulty, gain or loss. Because the Methodist has been set at liberty by God's Spirit, he finds his deepest satisfaction in doing God's will, on Earth even as it is in Heaven.

"The Methodist keeps *all* God's commandments—not halfheartedly, but with enthusiasm and gladness. The Methodist's obedience to God is in direct proportion to his love for God. And this 'perfect love' is the source of the Methodist's desire to obey God's Law one hundred percent. All this means that the Methodist is continually offering his whole self to God, holding back nothing, but giving all to increase the glory of God in the world.

"The Methodist knows that every single ability has come from God. So the Methodist gladly dedicates these talents to the Lord. The Methodist withholds nothing from God, nothing. Before he became a Christian, the Methodist allowed evil to take control of his body and his mind. Now, having died to the authority of sin, and having risen with Christ to a new and holy life, the Methodist has given himself over to God's control.

"Not only does the Methodist *aim* at complete dedication to God, he achieves this. His business, his recreation, his social life all serve this great purpose: 'Whatever you do, in word and deed, do it all in the name of the Lord

Jesus, giving thanks to God the Father through Him.'

"The customs of this world don't prevent the Methodist from full dedication to God. He runs the race for daily life, knowing that God has ordained this as his calling. The Methodist knows that wickedness is wrong in the sight of God, even though society may consider it perfectly acceptable. The Methodist never forgets that someday, everybody will have to give account to God for every thought and every action.

"Therefore, the Methodist cannot follow the crowd, when the crowd chooses to do evil. He cannot devote himself to selfish indulgence. The Methodist can no more be preoccupied with making money than he could swallow red-hot embers. Nor can the Methodist waste money on fancy clothes, or jewelry, which flatter the senses, but do not glorify God at all.

"Another mark of a Methodist: he will not take part in any amusement which has the least possibility of causing harm to others. He cannot speak evil of his neighbor any more than the Methodist can lie for God or any man. Love keeps guard over the Methodist's lips, so he cannot speak evil of anybody. Nor is God's precious gift of speech wasted with useless, inane chatter which does not help people in some constructive way.

"Whatever things are pure and noble, on these the Methodist fixes attention. Thus, all that the Methodist says or does somehow furthers the Gospel of Jesus Christ.

"As time permits, the Methodist does good to all, his neighbors and strangers; his friends and enemies. This includes every kind of good. Naturally, the Methodist provides food for the hungry, clothing to the naked. He visits people who are sick and in prison. But even more important than this, the Methodist labors to do good to the souls of men. According to the ability which God has given him, the Methodist labors to awaken those who have never known God, and therefore sleep the slumber of eternal death. And when men are awakened to God, the Methodist helps them realize that the atoning blood of Jesus has power to cleanse away their sins. The greatest good work a Methodist can do is to help somebody get into right relationship with God. For this is the only way a man can have peace with God.

"When the Methodist meets someone who has not yet found peace with God, the Methodist stirs him up in the hope that he may be set free to do the good works which God intends for every person to do.

"The Methodist is willing to spend his time and energies in doing this important work for God. His time and his talents are given as a loving sacrifice to God in order that the people round about him may grow into the fullness of Christ.

"These are the principles and practices of Methodism. These are the marks of a true Methodist. By these things alone does the Methodist wish to be distinguished from other men.

"Someone may say, 'Why, these are only the common, basic principles of Christianity!' This is what Methodism is, nothing more or less. We Methodists refuse to be distinguished from other men, by any other than the common principles of Christianity—the plain, old Christianity that I teach, renouncing and detesting all other marks of distinction. Any person who fits this pattern is a Christian no matter what you call him. It is not a matter of denominational label, but of being inwardly and outwardly conformed to the will of God, as this is revealed in the Bible.

"The Christian thinks, speaks, and lives according to the pattern set by Jesus. And his soul is renewed in righteousness and holiness, after God's own image.

"By these marks we Methodists labor to distinguish ourselves from the unbelieving world; from all whose minds and lives are not ruled according to the Gospel of Christ. But we Methodists do not wish to be distinguished at all from real Christians of any denomination. Like them, we are seeking that perfection of Christ which we have not yet attained. As Jesus said, whoever does the will of the Heavenly Father is our brother, sister, and mother.

"And so I beg you, let all true Christians remain united. Let us not be divided among ourselves. Is your heart right as my heart is with yours? I ask no further question; give me your hand. For the sake of mere opinions or terms, let us not destroy the work of God.

"Do you love God? This is enough. I give you the right hand of fellowship.

"If there is any consolation in Christ, any comfort in love, any fellowship in the Spirit, any affection and sympathy, then let us work together on behalf of the Gospel. Let us walk in a way that is worthy of the vocation to which we are called. Let us walk in lowliness and meekness with long-suffering, kindly sparing one another in love, trying always to keep the unity of the Spirit in the bond of peace. For we remember always, that there is one body, and one Spirit, one hope to our calling; one Lord, one faith, one baptism, one God and Father of us all. He is above all things, through all things, and in you as well."

QUESTIONS FOR DISCUSSION

1. *What does John Wesley identify as "the distinguishing marks" of a Methodist? Why does he spend so much time telling what they are not?*

2. *Many people quote Wesley as follows to prove that Methodists are free to believe just about anything: "But as to all opinions which do not strike at the root of Christianity, we think and let think." Does this give Methodists freedom to believe anything?*

3. *What is the Methodist meaning of "salvation" as given here?*

4. *Comment on Wesley's warning: "too many people make a religion out of (1) doing no harm or (2) doing good" (and often these two together). Have you known anybody whom this describes? How is this kind of religion different from Methodism as Wesley defined it in* Character of a Methodist?

5. *Today, there are many meanings of the word "love." How can it be defined on the basis of Wesley's teaching?*

6. *In your own words, describe the God whom Wesley says Methodists know as Father.*

7. *Describe the place which Jesus Christ plays in Methodist faith, as Wesley defines it here.*

8. *What work is done by the Holy Spirit, according to* Character of a Methodist?

9. *Do you think Methodists should believe in hell, on the basis of this historic Methodist teaching? Why—or why not?*

10. *From this material, what is the proper Methodist attitude toward suffering and tragedy?*

11. *Would you say it is possible for a Methodist to be "inactive" if he or she had the religion described in* Character of a Methodist? *Explain.*

12. *What is the source of inner purity for the Methodist?*

13

Putting It All Together

IN THESE TWELVE chapters we have looked at the historic faith of John Wesley and the early Methodists. We have tried to understand some of the most important ingredients of this faith—one of the most dynamic in the history of the Christian Church. And we have tried to suggest what this faith does and could mean to Methodists living in the closing years of the twentieth century.

Finally, it seems worthwhile to consider some of the ways that historic Methodist faith might change America —if Wesley's "Scriptural Christianity" was taken seriously. With some 10,000,000 calling themselves Methodists, the potential is very great—if these millions were touched and quickened by the same Spirit which warmed John Wesley's heart and changed his life.

There are many evidences of social and personal degeneration in America today. Some signs of the times: splitting up of many families; dramatically increasing crime rate among the very young; corruption and amorality in high places; indifference to people's suffering and to social injustice. Some are saying that it is the twilight of the American Dream; that we are slipping into some sort of dark morass as a nation, and as individuals.

In the early 1700s England was also sinking into national and individual degradation. Alcoholism was epidemic, for it offered the hopeless poor a way of anesthetizing themselves against the hopelessness of a society where the rich had no compassion for the poor. Indeed, historians have said that England was on a parallel course with France in the toboggan ride toward revolution. France had a revolution, England didn't. Some historians give the credit to the Methodist movement which gave many poor people a sense of hope, personal worth. Conversion of hundreds of thousands, rich and poor, changed countless family situations and made a difference across Great Britain. When Jesus Christ enters the lives of so many people something good is bound to happen.

The original Methodist idea is that society is composed of individuals. So you accomplish social change by changing the human derelicts into productive citizens. Thus Methodists saved people's bodies, homes, jobs, and self-respect—along with their souls.

However, the social change caused by original Methodism was a by-product of the main desire to "seek and save the lost." In seeking after personal salvation, the early Methodist found social transformation as a bonus. Wesley crusaded against slavery, alcoholism, and other social evils. But his main concern is revealed by a statement that he made many times to Methodist preachers: "You have one business and one business only: to save souls. Spend yourself in this work only and in none other."

The original Methodist idea was that as God changes people, society will be changed. For society is an interrelationship of people. Their aggregate human problems produce the complex of social, economic, cultural, and political problems. Today many people reject the idea that the church's main job is to change individuals spiritually, as the foundation for social change. Critics point to the so-called "Bible belt" where conversion has been preached and practiced for generations, with little apparent influence on social problems. And, say the critics, while all the camp meetings were going on in the 1800s, a continent was being stolen from the Indians under the banner of "manifest destiny." The Christians, apparently, saw nothing wrong in this.

Unfortunately, there is truth in these charges. To deny them is to ignore our history. But this simply shows how Methodism became Americanized and how it has evolved into something far different from the Methodism of John Wesley. Along the frontier, people were scattered thinly and few clergymen were available to act as spiritual leaders. So American Methodism rarely succeeded in making the continuing Wesleyan emphasis upon "growth in faith" within a close, disciplined community of believers. Under the influence of revivalism, American Methodism became more and more experience-centered, glorying in conversion as the end-all of religion when actually it is the first step only.

The results can be seen from something that happened in both North and South during the War Between the States. Methodist preachers sometimes concluded services with fervent exhortations to come to the altar—and join the Union or Confederate Army! No better expression can be found for the idea of Charles Ferguson, noted earlier, that Methodism has been the perfect reflection of American culture. The Methodism of John Wesley was as radically different from the prevailing culture as today's hippies are different from the middle-class American.

We have rarely, if ever, been radical enough in our Christianity. That is the trouble, and nothing less than radical following of Jesus Christ and His Gospel can deliver America from the deepening social and moral crisis that engulfs us.

Suppose the Christ type of self-giving love, emphasized in doctrine and life by John Wesley, became a real force in the homes of America's Methodist millions. Divorces would stop. Children's values would be conditioned more by Christ than by television. God's love would be demonstrated as "a more excellent way" than the way of materialism and self-centeredness. Fathers and mothers would provide children with Biblical models of what husband and wife should be. And through prayer God would work miracles, drawing families closer to each other and to Him.

The use of drugs, tobacco, and alcohol are signs of the addict's inner emptiness. When Christ enters a life, this emptiness is filled, so the crutches can be thrown away. The Jesus Revolution has proved this, liberating thousands of young adults from drugs. The established church did not liberate them, but Jesus did. This shows what can happen when the power of Jesus is brought to bear on social evils.

Crime, sexual deviation and promiscuity are a massive pileup of the individual problems of countless human beings. Get these human beings into Christ—and Christ into them—and sex will assume its proper place as God's precious gift, intended to enrich the radical and total commitment of one man to one woman, "till death do us part." The criminal will no longer steal if Christ is Lord of his or her life.

Consider the curse of materialism. Americans work frantically for more and more material things. Just paying the bills and maintaining our standard of living causes mothers to work outside the home and fathers to have two or even three jobs. Child neglect is often the result.

Suppose all Methodists decided to live by Wesley's teaching, "earn all you can, save all you can, give all you can." Think of the billions of dollars, now wasted on per-

133

sonal luxuries, which would be liberated for Christ's service. Churches would not have a problem raising money; the problem would be how to spend it all to God's best advantage.

Go down the list of social "problems" and Christ is the answer. But how, in a practical sense, can this remedy be applied?

Here is where the church comes in. God has ordained it to be the agency through which people make and maintain contact with the Living God. The first job of the church is to "make disciples" for Christ; then to nurture Christians so they will become more like Jesus Christ in daily life.

To do this will require a massive reversal of priorities. The church will have to get rid of its General Motors obsession for bigness. The church will have to stop endless tinkering with its internal machinery. It will have to realize that its one unique asset is not a bureaucracy or a large membership roll or fancy church buildings, but Jesus Christ. He must be emphasized, talked about and emulated ahead of everything.

The whole structure of seminary education must be revised to produce ministers who, like John Wesley, would be first concerned with the souls of men. Seminaries will have to stop majoring in philosophy, sociology, and churchmanship and begin majoring in Bible faith—the foundation for all that is really important.

The greatest readjustment will have to be made by the people who make up the church. By an act of divine grace, their idea of the church must be changed from that of a professionally run organization with no claim on their lives. Instead, they must realize that the church is a "priesthood of believers" and that every Christian is a minister. They will have to grow out of the bricks and mortar obsession. They will have to care more about Christ, the Gospel, and prayer, than beautiful church buildings and spacious parking lots. They will have to stop hiding from themselves, their neighbors, and God in the impersonality of big churches.

Perhaps big churches should be broken up into smaller congregations. In many cases this would mean pastors working full time on secular jobs, and sharing the work of ministry with laymen. And this will mean everyone putting Christ and His church ahead of television, lodges, weekends at the lake, and countless other "things." It will mean limiting church membership to serious Christians or seekers—probably dropping from the rolls two thirds of those now identified as Methodists. Once John Wesley said, "Give me ten members who fear nothing but God and hate only sin and I will turn England upside down." He did—but not with two thirds of the Methodists apathetic. It will mean getting close to other people, bearing their burdens, sharing time with them, money with them, homes with them. It may mean spending less time in our comfortable church buildings and more time on our knees in prayer and doing the faith out in the world. It may mean setting up one or more Wesley classes in every existing Methodist church.

The church as it now exists will not do the job. Methodists have had little if any constructive influence in America for many years. That is one reason why our nation is a pagan country with an increasingly thin and meaningless religious veneer.

We have, it seems, only two choices. Either we sit idly by and watch sin destroy America; or else we shall follow the leading of Jesus (and John Wesley) and get serious about the faith and get busy fighting the powers of evil. It is either-or with no alternatives.

The "little-faiths" contemplate the tangled skein of America's problems and say, "What's the use?" They throw up their hands and surrender to the enemy of everything that God wishes us (and America) to become.

But real Methodists know that the power Jesus gives them is greater than the world.

Real Methodists know that on the Cross and by His Resurrection, Jesus has already defeated evil. He has promised His followers power to accomplish even greater works than He Himself has done.

Real Methodists believe that Gospel truth is stronger than the world's evil. "Though the wrong be oft so strong, God is the ruler yet."

Real Methodists know that God has always worked miracles through a small and dedicated minority, that God and one make a majority.

Real Methodists realize that only Christ and the Gospel are eternal; that all else is subject to constant change and flux. Therefore the real Methodist is not threatened by changing forms of the church, changing modes of transmitting the Gospel, cultures that change from boyhood or girlhood days. Being firmly rooted and grounded on the Eternal, the real Methodist is the most practical, flexible, audacious kind of person. He or she is not paralyzed by "future shock" because the real Methodist knows Him who holds the future.

Real Methodists realize the lateness of the hour; that the Lord may return at any moment, ending the opportunities to bring many out of eternal darkness into everlasting life.

Our life is a dream,
  Our time as a stream
Glides swiftly away,
  Glides swiftly away,
And the fugitive moment
  Refuses to stay.

Oh that each in the day
  Of His coming may say
I have fought my way through
  I have finished the work
Thou didst give me to do.—*Charles Wesley*

QUESTIONS FOR DISCUSSION

1. *If you have read the previous chapters, you should have a good idea of the kind of faith held by Wesley and the early Methodists. Does it appeal to you? Or would you say it has no real meaning for Christians living in the modern world?*

2. *How can we explain the present decline in American morals and society?*

3. *How was the England John Wesley knew in the 1700s the same as America today? How was it different?*

4. *What happened to Methodism when it came from England to America? How did the frontier affect it? Describe the differences between Methodism as it developed in America from the original of Wesley.*

5. *What was the historic Methodist thinking about the way to change society? Is this a popular view in American Methodism today? If not, what is the difference?*

6. *What about people who say it does no good to try to improve society by changing individuals? How about their claim that all the evangelism and conversions of the Bible Belt and frontier did not prevent injustice to blacks and Indians?*

7. *Do you agree with the statement that churches as they are presently organized and operating have not done the job of influencing America for God?*

8. *What changes did this chapter suggest that the church organization would have to make in order to be following the "Scriptural Christianity" of John Wesley?*

9. *How will seminaries need to change?*

10. *What changes were suggested for local churches, in order to have them in line with original Methodism?*

11. *Comment on the statement that the problem of American Methodists is that they have not been radical enough. Was Jesus radical? John Wesley?*

12. *In your opinion, why haven't Methodists and Methodist churches made more impact upon the lives of their members, their communities, and the nation?*

BIBLIOGRAPHY

Cannon, William R. **The Theology of John Wesley.** Nashville: Abingdon, 1946.

Church, Leslie F. **Knight of the Burning Heart.** Nashville: Abingdon-Cokesbury, undated.

Deschner, John. **Wesley's Christologian Interpretation.** Dallas: Southern Methodist University Press, 1960.

Ensley, Francis Gerald. **John Wesley, Evangelist.** Nashville: Tidings, 1955.

Faulkner, John Alfred. **Wesley as Sociologist, Theologian, Churchman.** Cincinnati: Methodist Book Concern, 1918.

Ferguson, Charles W. **Organizing to Beat the Devil.** New York City: Doubleday, 1971.

Fitchett, W. H. **Wesley and His Century.** Cincinnati: Jennings & Graham, 1912.

Geiger, Kenneth (compiler). **Further Insights into Holiness.** Kansas City: Beacon Hill Press, 1963.

Hilderbrandt, Franz (ed). **Wesley Hymn Book.** London: A. Weeks & Co., 1960.

Holmes, D. **The Wesley Offering.** New York: Derby & Miller. 1852.

Joy, James Richard. **John Wesley's Awakening.** Cincinnati: Methodist Book Concern, 1937.

Kay, J. Alan. **Fifty Hymns by Charles Wesley.** London: Epworth Press, 1957.

Kennedy, Gerald. **The Marks of a Methodist.** Nashville: Methodist Evangelistic Materials, 1960.

Keysor, Charles W. **John Wesley.** Elgin, Illinois: David C. Cook Publishing Co., 1966.

Lindstrom, Harold. **Wesley and Sanctification.** Nashville: Abingdon Press, 1946.

Marston, Bishop Leslie Ray. **From Age to Age a Living Witness.** Winona Lake, Indiana: Light & Life Press, 1960.

McConnell, Francis J. **John Wesley.** New York: Abingdon Press, 1939.

Norwood, Frederick A. **Church Membership in the Methodist Tradition.** Nashville: Methodist Publishing House, 1958.

Nygaard, Norman E. **Bishop on Horseback.** Grand Rapids: Zondervan Publishing House, 1962.

Outler, Albert C., editor. **John Wesley.** New York: Oxford University Press, 1964.

Schmidt, Martin. **John Wesley: A Theological Biography.** Nashville: Abingdon Press, 1962.

Stokes, Mack B. **Major Methodist Beliefs.** Nashville: Methodist Publishing House, 1960.

The Book of Discipline of the United Methodist Church. Nashville: Methodist Publishing House, 1968.

The History of American Methodism. Nashville: Abingdon Press, 1964.

The Methodist Hymnal. Nashville: Methodist Publishing House, 1964.

Watson, Philip S. **The Message of the Wesleys.** New York: Macmillan Company, 1964.

Wesley, John. **A Plain Account of Christian Perfection.** London: Epworth Press, 1952.

Wesley, John. **Explanatory Notes on the New Testament.** London: Wesleyan Conference Office, undated.

Wesley, John. **Journals.** London: J. M. Dent, 1922.

Wesley, John. **The Character of a Methodist (paraphrase).** Elgin, Illinois: Good News, 1967.

Williams, Colin W. **John Wesley's Theology Today.** Nashville: Abingdon Press, 1960.

Wood, A. Skevington. **The Burning Heart: John Wesley, Evangelist.** Grand Rapids: Eerdmans Publishing Co., 1967.

Wynkoop, Mildred Bangs. **A Theology of Love (The Dynamic of Wesleyanism).** Kansas City: Beacon Hill Press, 1972.

Wyon, Olive. **Teachings Toward Christian Perfection.** New York: W.S.C.S., Board of Missions, The Methodist Church, 1963.

Yates, Arthur S. **The Doctrine of Assurance.** London: Epworth Press, 1952.

If you've just finished this book, we think you'll agree . . .

A COOK PAPERBACK IS

REWARDING READING

Try some more!

HOW SILENTLY, HOW SILENTLY by Joseph Bayly. Fantastic entertainment . . . with meaning YOU decide! Thirteen tales of mystery, drama, humor, science fiction lead to discovery.
73304—$1.25

FAITH AT THE TOP by Wesley Pippert. From a seasoned Washington reporter . . . a look at 10 eminently successful people who dared to bring Christ with them all the way.
75796—$1.50

LOOK AT ME, PLEASE LOOK AT ME by Clark, Dahl and Gonzenbach. Accepting the retarded—with love—as told in the moving struggle of two women who learned how.
72595—$1.25

THE 13TH AMERICAN by Pastor Paul. Every 13th American is an alcoholic, and it could be anyone. A sensitive treatment of alcoholism by a minister who fought his way back.
72629—$1.50

THE EVIDENCE THAT CONVICTED AIDA SKRIPNIKOVA edited by Bourdeaux and Howard-Johnston. Religious persecution in Russia! The story of a young woman's courage.
72652—$1.25

LET'S SUCCEED WITH OUR TEENAGERS by Jay Kesler. Substitutes hope for parental despair—offers new understanding that exposes the roots of parent-child differences.
72660—$1.25

THE PROPHET OF WHEAT STREET by James English. Meet William Borders, a Southern Black educated at Northwestern University, who returned to lead the black church in Atlanta.
72678—$1.25

WHAT A WAY TO GO! by Bob Laurent. Your faith BEYOND church walls. Laurent says, "Christianity is not a religion, it's a relationship." Freedom, new life replace dull routine!
72728—$1.25

THE VIEW FROM A HEARSE (new enlarged edition) by Joseph Bayly. Examines suicide. Death can't be ignored—what is the Christian response? Hope is as real as death.
73270—$1.25